D1168519

3 5109 0008 1885 4

785.0903
C23o

THE ORCHESTRA IN THE XVIIIth CENTURY

FROM "THE MODERN MUSICK-MASTER," 1730.

The Orchestra
IN THE XVIIIth CENTURY

ADAM CARSE

Fellow of the Royal Academy of Music

1969

BROUDE BROTHERS LIMITED
NEW YORK

Reprinted by arrangement with
W. Heffer & Sons Limited, Cambridge

Printed in Great Britain

PREFACE

The ground covered in these pages has hardly been touched in English, and only partially in German by Mennicke and Schünemann, and in French by Cucuel and Brenet.

Information about 18th century orchestras must obviously come from contemporary sources. These sources are not many, nor very explicit, for those who wrote about music in the 18th century, like their 19th and 20th century successors, have always been more ready to devote their attention to individuals and their works than to corporate bodies and their playing. In a mass of biographical, critical and analytical matter it is only rarely that the investigator is able to retrieve scraps of information, usually given incidentally, on which to build up the story of the development of the orchestra during the period in which it made its most vital growth. Histories of music, of musicians and of musical instruments cover a wide and ever expanding field, but the growth of that great composite instrument, the orchestra, has been so neglected by historians that it has always been difficult to know where to turn for information.

In the following pages the attempt has been made to piece together the story of how the orchestra grew, from its infancy at the end of the 17th century to its adolescence at the end of the 18th century, to recover and collect the widely scattered matter on which alone such a story could be based, and at the same time to co-ordinate the evolution of the performing body with that of its expression through the medium of orchestration.

For kind help in the labour of research the author is much indebted to his friends W. F. H. Blandford, Esq., R. B. Chatwin, Esq., R. Morley Pegge, Esq., and especially to Lyndesay G. Langwill, Esq., and Geoffrey Sharp, Esq., for invaluable help in reading the proofs.

ADAM CARSE.

Great Missenden, 1940.

CONTENTS

NOTE

In order to avoid the frequent repetition in these pages of long titles of books, they are referred to by their authors' names. The full titles will be found in the Bibliography.

CHAPTER I

INTRODUCTION

As a preliminary to an investigation of the orchestra in the 18th century it will be well to make some attempt to see the music of that period as nearly as possible as it was seen by those who lived at that time, and to try to get into closer touch with the conditions under which 18th century musicians worked.

It is obvious that we cannot hear the music of so long ago just in the same way that it was heard in its own time. We cannot get rid of experiences which we have had, and therefore cannot completely blot out from our minds all that we know of 19th century music. If it were possible to skip over the intervening century, to banish its influence and eradicate its effect on our point of view, we should be in a better position to understand the music of the 18th century. But that cannot be done. The 19th century music stands between us and that of the 18th century; we cannot ignore or remove it.

The best we can do is to make a determined effort to remember how much has come between us and the musicians of the 18th century. We can keep on reminding ourselves that what to us is the past was to them the future; that we are looking back on what they were looking forward to; that we, merely owing to our having lived at a later period, enjoy the great advantage over them that we know all about what they could only speculate about.

In fairness to the 18th century musicians, if we would understand them and their music, we must attempt to forget some of our accumulated knowledge and experience. We must try to abandon some of our conceptions of music, and retain only those which the musicians of the 18th century could have shared fairly with us.

We might begin by ceasing to view 18th century music and musicians as we view the objects in a museum or an antique shop. We are apt to look back on that period as one in which people had quaint and rather artificial manners, and moved about

1

in pretty costumes like actors on a stage. We see them framed in a proscenium which discloses only the picturesque, the romantic or the adventurous sides of their lives. They were so delightfully old-fashioned, so quaint, so stilted, so vulgar and so "18th century." The musicians, dressed in fancy clothes, wearing powdered wigs and girt with swords, move about in an unreal and stage-like world, posing for our amusement. We see the charming façade of the Georgian house, but not its primitive sanitation. We have to remember that the musicians of the 18th century were living, not in the past, but in the present. To themselves they were not objects of historical interest; they were not actors in a period play, posing for the benefit of future generations. Even if every condition of life has changed, human nature remains as it was, and the 18th century musicians were human beings, most of them very ordinary human beings, living for their own benefit, striving to make money and achieve fame while they lived, very much as do the musicians of the present day. Those which we call the "great composers" of the 18th century didn't picture themselves raised far above their fellows, crowned with a special aureole, the elect of many generations, immortalised and almost deified.

As soon as we get into touch with their personalities and their lives we see how they struggled to make a living by pleasing their patrons or their public, and how they worked for their own welfare with little thought of their future reputations.

We shall get a little nearer to the 18th century, its music and its musicians, if we can view them at closer quarters, without the picturesque setting which distracts our attention and hides from us the practical matter-of-fact way in which the art of music was cultivated and carried on.

Another conception which we might try to get rid of is the idea that the music of the 18th century was dominated by the work of a few great composers, more especially the notion that the whole structure rested on the work of four great German composers— Bach, Handel, Haydn and Mozart. Incidentally, we might break the bonds with which we have tied Bach to Handel and Haydn to Mozart, and have doomed them to run in pairs in an everlasting three-legged race along the course of musical history. These four, each in their own time, within their own spheres and independently of each other, were all prominent German composers. Neither was unrecognised or neglected in his own time, and the music of only one of them, Bach, went temporarily out of fashion after the composer's death. But all of them had to share their position in German music with a great many others who were regarded either as their equals or as running them very close. The great four were not yet placed on pedestals so high that their feet were well above the heads of all other composers of their time; their superiority was not so overwhelming that they appeared as giants amongst hundreds of pigmies. The real music of the 18th century was that of hundreds of composers, good, bad and indifferent, German, French, Italian and English, whose names alone would fill many of these pages. They all worked, not for the approval of posterity, but for their own good. The bulk of their music served its purpose and has passed into oblivion, while we, for our present use, merely skim the cream off the whole output.

If we dip into the musical literature written after the middle of the century we get a closer and a truer view of the situation as it really was than if we form our judgment on the limited selection of 18th century music which is now played, or even on the histories of music in which the attention is focussed almost entirely on the very few composers whose work has endured.

Obviously we cannot expect to hear much of Haydn or Mozart before the last quarter of the century; but we may expect to hear how the composers of the generation of Bach and Handel and their immediate successors were regarded by their contemporaries.

The composer "Bach" is often mentioned by writers in the 'seventies and 'eighties, and we have to get accustomed to discover without surprise that they were writing about, not Johann Sebastian Bach, but about one of his sons, generally Carl Philipp Emanuel or else Johann Christian. J. S. Bach had always been recognised as an outstanding organist and a clever contrapuntist, but the style of his music was getting out of date after the mid-century: "He composed many pieces, both for the church and the chamber, but all in such a heavy style that they are rarely played nowadays."[1] An anonymous writer[2] in 1779 gave a list of the most important German composers of the century up till that time; they include: Handel, Telemann, Stölzel, K. H. Graun, Hasse, J. S. Bach, C. P. E. Bach, J. C. Bach, Franz Benda, Georg

[1] Schubart, p. 63.

[2] Writing under the pseudonym *einem teutschen Biedermann*—a German upright honest man (p. 7).

Benda, Quantz, Kirnberger, Agricola, Schwanberger, Homilius, Holzbauer, Cannabich, Hiller, Wolf, Naumann, Gluck, Schweitzer, Rolle "and others." We note that he included J. S. Bach, Handel and Gluck in his roll of honour, and wonder what some of the other names were doing there. Burney's review of German music[1] brings forward the names of over eighty composers who were deemed worthy of mention, a catalogue which includes the few whose music we know, many that we know by name, and some that have not been able to keep their places even in our musical dictionaries. In 1784 Forkel[2] gave the names of over 340 composers then living in Germany, and the pages of Marpurg and others could all contribute yet more names to the lengthy list of those who were making music in Germany during the 18th century. But a collection of names is not very helpful, except that it would give us some idea of how many musical oysters have to be opened in order to find one pearl.

If to a list of the German makers of music we were to add one which included the names of all the Italian composers who worked during the 18th century, we should have to add many more pages to our musical directory, for Italy produced whole litters of composers every year without ever showing any signs of exhaustion. The records of French music are also full of composers' names, some of which we recognise as the composers of music which turns up sporadically in our programmes, but most of which we can hardly associate with any music that we ever hear. An English, a Spanish and a Netherlands list would fill up a few more pages, and the grand total would give us several hundreds of composers who provided the 18th century with its music. It would include the mere handful whose music is now part of our regular repertoire, and the very small proportion of the total number whose works are occasionally dug up and offered to us as period pieces or samples of this or that school or nationality.

If in the contemporary records of the 18th century we do not always find the composers placed in the order of merit exactly as we have since arranged them, we need not be surprised at the apparent lack of discrimination, for it is a most hazardous business trying to assess the lasting quality of any composer's work while his style is still current or not long out of date. Unquestionably, it is much easier now to distinguish between the

---

[1] History, II, p. 941.
[2] *Almanach*, 1784 (*Verzeignisz jetztlebender Componisten in Deutschland*), p. 53.

quality of the work of tweedledum and tweedledee (Handel and Buononcini)[1] than it was in 1732. It is not fair to write down Schubart an ass because he told us that J. S. Bach's music was a bit on the heavy side in the 'eighties, that Telemann "became one of the best composers in Europe," that Jommelli was "the first composer in the world," and that Georg Benda was "one of the greatest composers who ever lived—one of the epoch-makers of our time."[2] Nor need we reckon Junker a fool because he apostrophised Carl Stamitz as: "the elect amongst thousands; how sensitive, how inimitable and heartfelt is the grace of your music. Posterity will see in you the birth of a new epoch of taste, and will bless you because you were so industrious."[3] Burney cannot be dismissed as a writer of nonsense because he found both "fire and genius" in the symphonies of Johann Stamitz.[4] If Georg Benda and Carl Stamitz did not eventually turn out to be exactly epoch-makers; if we now find Telemann's music a bit dry, Jommelli's a bit empty, and Johann Stamitz's rather dull, we cannot afford to be hard on Schubart, Junker and Burney, because we cannot be sure that we are not writing exactly the same sort of thing to-day about present-day composers whose music has no more chance of enduring life than was granted to that of Telemann, Jommelli, Benda and the Stamitz father and son.

If we are to believe all that we read about the music of to-day, there are enough "great," "distinguished" or "famous" composers alive at this moment to provide the world with masterpieces for the rest of time. If amongst the hundreds of composers who were busy in the 18th century a mere half-dozen have turned out to be stayers, can we hope that we have several dozens of winners running to-day? Because we have knighted the great Smith and play his works constantly, it does not follow that a note of his will be heard 200 years hence. Even though we are thrilled by the music of the late Brown, and have made busts of him and have written books about him, we cannot be sure that his name will be found in the 50th edition of Grove,

---

[1] This refers to John Byrom's epigram (Rockstro, p. 182):
"Some say, compar'd to Buononcini,
That Mynheer Handel's but a ninny;
Others aver that he to Handel
Is scarcely fit to hold a candle.
Strange all this difference should be
'Twixt tweedledum and tweedledee."
[2] *Aesthetik*, pp. 63, 103, 19, 75. [3] *Almanach*, 1782, p. 57. [4] History, II, p. 945.

c. 2140. Although we think nothing of the music of the wretched Robinson, and never give him a decent performance, that is no guarantee that his works will not fill our concert-rooms early in the 22nd century. Posterity cares nothing for the reputation a composer enjoyed during his lifetime; it brushes away changes of taste and fashion, and ignores contemporary opinion; it makes its own selection in its own deliberate and sure way, and will have nothing but the pick of the music of any period in its permanent repertoire.

Before that final selection is made, many composers have to come and go; but in the meantime they do provide the music of their own time, even though they are eventually wiped off the slate as completely as if they had never been there. The process of selecting the best music works slowly, so we need not be surprised when we find that in the contemporary records of 18th century music the names Bach, Handel, Haydn and Mozart do not occur any more frequently than dozens of others which are now little more than history-book names. Burney told us that "the composers to be found in Milan are innumerable,"[1] and from Schubart we learn that "Paris swarms with musicians."[2]

If the 18th century produced a large crop of composers, its fertility in that respect was well matched by the fecundity of each composer. From Quantz[3] we learn that Ales. Scarlatti wrote about 4000 works, and Telemann still more. According to Burney,[4] Telemann had written 600 overtures by the year 1740, and Hasse's works were so many that the composer himself had lost count of them. Holzbauer is credited with 205 symphonies and concertos,[5] and J. G. Graun with 96 symphonies.[6] This rate of production was high and necessitated quick work. Dittersdorf finished three symphonies and a concerto within a month,[7] and "complying with the repeated requests of the directors, I wrote two more operas in German and one in Italian, all in the space of seven months."[8] The 18th century composer scorned to write one symphony or one concerto; he turned them out in batches of six or more. He composed a group of pieces, made what he could out of them, and then started to write some more, just as a craftsman makes an article, sells it, and then begins to make another.

[1] Present State (Italy), p. 105.   [2] Schubart, p. 160.
[3] Autob., Marpurg, I, p. 229.   [4] Present State (Germany), II, p. 243.
[5] Klob, p. 12.   [6] Mennicke, p. 536.   [7] Autob., p. 97.   [8] *Ibid.*, p. 256.

The 18th century composer often composed for a salary,[1] in fact, if he was a *Kapellmeister* he was engaged, not only to direct the performance of music for his employer, but also to compose it; and what he composed became the property of his employer or patron. Sometimes he presented some pieces to a likely patron and chanced what he got for them, hoping that it would be a cash payment rather than a gilt snuff-box. At other times he accepted a commission to compose at a fixed tariff. Gassmann wrote for Count Dietrichstein at the regular rate of 100 ducats for six symphonies or six quartets,[2] and was not allowed to let anyone else have a copy of them. At the Paris *Opéra* in the 'eighties the composer was paid 100 *livres* for each of the first ten performances of his opera, and 50 *livres* for each of the next 20, after which he derived no further benefit from it.[3] The regular rate for an opera produced in Vienna in the 'eighties was 100 ducats.[4]

The "employed" composer in the 18th century had to compose whatever his patron wanted. Almost everything was written to order and for a particular body of performers; nearly all 18th century music was "occasional music." When Haydn was asked why he had not written any quintets, his answer was: "Because nobody has ordered any."[5]

These conditions tended to make for a continuous production of new music, for a composer lost his pecuniary interest in a piece as soon as it was disposed of. It should also be remembered that a large output was necessary because at that time they had no accumulation of the instrumental music of over two centuries from which to choose a repertoire. Hardly any but 18th century music was played in the 18th century; it had to be made, so to speak, as they went along. When a prince set up a musical establishment he could not just order a lot of scores and parts from a music-seller; he had to employ a *Kapellmeister* to compose music for him. He kept him for the purpose of supplying music just as we keep hens to lay eggs for us. If an employer wanted a change of music, he commissioned another composer to write something for him, and that composer wrote the pieces to order for a cash payment and for the exclusive use of the purchaser. Music did not circulate as freely nor so quickly as it

---

[1] Mozart offered to compose for a salary (Letter, Aug. 8, 1786).
[2] Hanslick, p. 44.   [3] Marpurg, I, p. 188.
[4] Dittersdorf, p. 256.   Jahn, I, p. 652.   [5] Hanslick, p. 40.

may now; much of it was anchored to a particular place, and remained there unless a MS. copy of it was made and sent elsewhere.

When a composer was not regularly employed, he hawked his music about wherever he thought he could find a market for it. He might produce it himself, exploit it at his own risk and speculate on the result.   He ran himself as a business concern, as Handel did in London.   In either case, he was always writing for some definite performance.   He was not writing for the world in general, as the modern composer does, or likes to think he is doing.

If it is asked: what rights had the 18th century composer in his work?   The answer would seem to be—very few, if any.   The only way he could prevent anyone else from exploiting his work was to make sure that nobody could get hold of a copy of it. Once a piece was put down on paper there was nothing to prevent anyone producing or even publishing it who could get a copy of it.   Copyists and sellers of music unblushingly advertised and sold unauthorised MSS. or printed copies of pieces right under the eyes of the composer, who had no redress.   In Italy, the copyists at the theatres enjoyed special privileges when a new work was produced: "The copyist is absolutely delighted, which is a good omen in Italy, where, if the music is a success, the copyist by selling the arias sometimes makes more money than the *Kapellmeister* does by his composition."[1]   Mozart was always scheming to dodge the unscrupulous copyists and publishers who were ever ready to exploit the young composer's work for their own gain, and if he was sometimes outwitted, he was quite ready to give as good as he got: "Le Gros[2] purchased from me the two overtures and the sinfonia concertante.   He thinks that he alone has them, but he is wrong, for they are still fresh in my mind, and, as soon as I get home, I shall write them down again."[3]

The arrangements for publishing music in the 18th century were such as would make the flesh of the modern composer creep.   If any law held good, it was the law of the jungle. Whether he had acquired it by fair means or foul, the one who gained most was the one who was the first to publish a work. When Mozart was busy making a piano arrangement of his

[1] Leopold Mozart's letter, Dec. 15, 1770.
[2] Director of the *Concert spirituel* in Paris.   [3] Mozart's letter, Oct. 3, 1778.

"Entführung" for the publisher Torricella, and when the first act had been engraved, it was discovered that another arrangement of it by Stark had already been published by Schott in Mayence.[1] The composer sometimes sold his work to a publisher for a cash payment,[2] (one might almost say that he sold it by weight!) but that did not necessarily prevent him from offering the same work to another publisher, nor, apparently, did a publisher see any reason why he should not publish a work, if he could get a copy of it, without making any payment to the composer. In order to protect his own interest the composer often had his work engraved and published at his own expense, and was not ashamed to sell copies to the public at his own house. But even then he evidently didn't feel quite safe: "If I have some work printed or engraved at my own expense, how can I protect myself from being cheated by the engraver? For surely he can print off as many copies as he likes and therefore swindle me?"[3]

These smash and grab methods held good until copyright laws were instituted during the early part of the 19th century.

The 18th century composer was always writing for the moment; he wrote much and quickly, and sought to gain what advantage he could from his work while it was new, before it circulated and became common property. This helps to explain why so much was written, why one work followed another in quick succession, and also why so much of the 18th century music is little more than hack-work turned out without much thought and given little finish. Even so, most of it served some definite purpose; it provided for present consumption in its day, and in the end the best of it went to build up a repertoire. If much of it was ephemeral, nearly all of it did live for a little while; there was little stillborn music in those days; less than there is now.

All these things should be remembered when we look back on the music of the 18th century through 20th century glasses. We cannot fairly judge the musicians of the past without taking into consideration the conditions under which they lived and worked.

When we narrow down our view of 18th century music and musicians, and focus our attention only on the orchestras and

[1] Leopold Mozart's letters, Mar. 12, 1785, and Dec. 16, 1785.

[2] Haydn offered the London publisher Will. Forster six symphonies and six quartets for 25 guineas (Pohl, II, p. 92).

[3] Mozart's letter, Feb. 20, 1784.

orchestral music of that period, some of our present-day conceptions must be modified, and others must be abandoned altogether.

An orchestra as we know it now, and an orchestra as it was known then, are not quite the same thing. We know it as a fully grown thing; they were witnessing its growth. Disregarding small bodies of players, or any which for various reasons are incomplete, the orchestra of to-day has a constitution which has long been stabilised and standardised. The main body is a combination of three self-contained groups of instruments, namely, the bowed-string group, the wood-wind and the brass groups. The main body is supplemented by a less essential fringe of percussion and plucked-string instruments, and a few outgrowths in the wood-wind and brass groups are added or withdrawn without materially altering the general constitution of these sections. At no time in the 18th century would that definition have held good. During that period the main body of the orchestra was still in the process of formation. The foundation or base on which it was built up consisted of one or more keyboard or chordal instruments; to that was added a more or less complete bowed-string group, a small and rather variable wood-wind group which was barely harmonically self-supporting, and on occasion a small brass group which could not provide its own harmony. By the end of the century the original basis, the keyboard and chordal instruments, had been almost entirely discarded; the bowed-string group had taken their place as the foundation of the body; the wood-wind group had become harmonically self-contained, and the brass group was still growing and remained as yet harmonically incomplete. For the greater part of the century, however, the keyboard and chordal instruments formed the centre around which the other groups grew and played, and from which the whole was largely controlled.

When looking back on the orchestras of the 18th century it is important to keep in mind the essential part played by the keyboard and chordal instruments, and to realise how much composers relied on these instruments to supply the harmony for their music. We must imagine the composers conceiving their music in melodic outline for bowed-string instruments against a harmonic background built up on an all-important general or universal bass part, the *basso continuo*.

We must not expect to find in the 18th century, especially in the earlier part, that clear distinction which we now make between chambei music and orchestral music; indeed, it is rather difficult to draw the line between a small orchestra in the 18th century and a party of chamber-music players. When the "Biedermann," already quoted, informs us that one cannot have an orchestra of less than four players, and that these should be one 1st violin, one 2nd violin, one viola and one 'cello,[1] we would like to ask him, if that is an orchestra, what is a string quartet? and how can we tell one from the other? The size of an orchestra, he said, should correspond to the size of the room in which it is playing. The old German writers make a clear distinction between church music, opera, and chamber music, but by the latter term they mean both orchestral music and what we now call chamber music. To them, chamber music was the instrumental music of a court, which was played in the chamber or private apartment of a sovereign or ruling prince.[2] The musicians attached to a court were *Kammermusiker*. Quantz (1752) too, regarded chamber music as that which was played in a room, whether by one or several players to each part.[3] The prefix "chamber" (*Kammer, camera*) in the 18th century should be understood rather as a term which was used to differentiate between private and public music-making.

One of the things that must be completely cut out of the picture of the 18th century orchestra is our conception of the orchestral conductor. The time-beating, interpretative orchestral conductor did not exist. The methods of directing instrumental performance in the 18th century will be more fully treated in a subsequent chapter; in the meantime it should be understood that the word "conductor" was applied to the musician who was in charge of a performance, but that orchestras were not controlled by a time-beating conductor.

All 18th century musicians were executants. There were none who were merely directors of performance, and none who were only composers of music. It was left to the 19th century to bring into being conductors and composers of music who did not combine these activities with actual playing on an instrument or singing. Most composers were instrumentalists, very often

[1] P. 36.
[2] See Koch. *Lexikon* (1802), arts. *Kammermusik* and *Kammermusikus*.
[3] *Versuch* XVII, sec. I, par. 15.

competent on both a keyboard and a bowed-string instrument, and not a few cases of composer-vocalists occur.[1] Virtuosi, of course, specialised each in their particular line, but never so exclusively nor to the extent that they do nowadays. Practical musicianship was expected of everyone, although, then as now, less musicianship was expected of vocalists, and least of all of Italian singers.[2] Just as all composers were executants, so nearly all executants were composers. There was hardly an instrumental soloist that didn't write and play his own solos. The travelling virtuoso carried about with him a bundle of his own concertos and sonatas, and he was reckoned a poor musician who couldn't compose his own repertoire. Quantz (1752) tells us that it was considered nothing to be able to write a solo piece: "Almost every instrumentalist does so. If he has no inventive powers, he uses borrowed ideas. If he doesn't know the rules of composition, he gets someone else to fill in the bass part for him. Thus it is that, instead of good examples, so many abortions make their appearance."[3]

The repertoire of German court orchestras consisted largely of works by its own *Kapellmeister*, and the operas produced in one place were generally the work of one or two composers who were on the spot and directed the performance of their own work. Thus, of the 33 operas produced in Berlin between 1742 and 1754, 26 were by Graun (Frederick the Great's *Kapellmeister*), four by Hasse, two by Nichelmann and one by Agricola.[4] Hasse composed most of the operas produced at Dresden while he was *Kapellmeister* to the King of Poland, and Jommelli supplied the bulk of those at Stuttgart when he was in charge of the Duke of Würtemberg's musical establishment. Even though the opera was not entirely a court affair, as for example, in Italy, Paris or London, the works produced were those of composers who were settled in these places, either permanently or temporarily, and wrote for the resources of the particular theatre. They were, or became for the time being, local composers. At the *Opéra* in Paris, for example, of the 105 operas and ballets produced between 1700 and 1750, all were by French, or, one might even say, by Parisian composers, except three by the German-born

---

[1] Mattheson, K. H. Graun, Hasse.

[2] "When accompanying conceited Italian women singers, one must be prepared to skip half bars in order to save them from disgrace" (Leopold Mozart, *Versuch*, XII, par. 20).

[3] *Versuch*, XVIII, par. 46.   [4] Marpurg, I, p. 80.

Batistin.[1] Similarly, at the Venetian theatres, between 1700 and 1730, no less than 270 operas were produced[2] of which all but four were composed by Italian musicians who either lived in Venice or went there for a period for the purpose of composing and producing operas.[3] On the whole, it might be said that, during the greater part of the 18th century, the performance of a musical work was generally associated with the composer's presence at the place where it was played, and that as far as possible he was the interpreter of his own music.

The clear distinction which has since grown up between "music" and "light music" hardly existed in the 18th century. The most distinguished of musicians composed and took part in the performance of dance music, out-door music and music played during meals. Court orchestras were at the same time the equivalents of the modern concert-orchestra, the theatre orchestra, the dance band, the restaurant band and the open-air promenade band. The same composers wrote the music for all of them. They were not divided into sheep and goats, highbrows and lowbrows, composers of art-music and trade-music. A composer didn't lose caste when his music became popular, in fact, he gained prestige thereby, and tried to make it popular. Secular music was intended to entertain and please; the 18th century composer knew better than to try to educate his audience; he aimed at pleasing them. Mozart's letters make it very clear that he was constantly striving to write in such a manner as would please his listeners locally, in Italy, in Paris, in Munich or Vienna, or wherever he went. Handel was not trying to educate his London audiences; he was trying to please them; and we may be sure that Haydn would not have kept his job in the Esterhazy household for so long if he had always written above the head of the prince. We cannot picture an 18th century Italian opera audience, the ruling prince of a German state, the Paris aristocracy, the "quality" or "haut ton" of 18th century London being taught musical appreciation by any composer. They would soon have sent about his business anyone who had tried to do so. The 18th century composer who claimed that he was writing for future generations would have been considered a lunatic; he

[1] Joh. Baptist Stuck, known in France as Jean Batistin.
[2] Marpurg, II, p. 493.
[3] One of the exceptions was Handel's *Agrippina*; the others were two by Heinichen and one by Hasse, who, although German-born, was practically an Italian composer.

wrote for the present, and didn't set himself to make the "classics" of the future.

In the 18th century the orchestra was only part, and not the most important part of a musical organisation. It existed at first rather as an adjunct to vocal or solo music; as an accompanying medium which supported the voices in church music and opera, or the instrumental soloist in the concerto. By the end of the century, however, the orchestra had gained sufficient independence and importance to be in a position to begin to challenge the supremacy of the vocal element which had hitherto been the dominating power in music.

For the greater part of the century the opera overture was nothing more than a preliminary to the main effort; something which could be talked through while the audience was settling down to listen to the performance they had come to hear. In spite of the efforts of Gluck to make the overture an integral part of the drama, and notwithstanding the fine overtures of Mozart towards the end of the century, most of them, and especially those by Italian composers, were carelessly and hastily put together. Quantz's opinion was that the Italian opera overtures (*sinfonia*) were generally made up of unwanted remains, used as a painter might use up the colours left on his palette to make a background for his picture.[1] Concerning the Italian overtures near the end of the century, Parke wrote: "The Italian composers of that day considered the overture to an opera of so little consequence that they generally left it till the last moment, and I have frequently known that scarcely time has been allowed for the copyist to get it ready for the last rehearsal."[2]

When, round about the middle of the century, the overture, detached from its opera, became the starting point and model for the concert-symphony, the status of the orchestra began to improve a little. The hundreds of symphonies which were printed during the second half of the century are evidence enough of a growing interest in purely orchestral music as such, and beginning to free itself from a position which had kept it always more or less in subjection to vocal music. Symphonies were then played at every concert; generally two or three at each concert. But the programmes of those days show the place of honour still allotted to the vocal or the instrumental solo. The symphony would always begin and end the concert, or the two halves of the

[1] *Versuch*, XVIII, par. 43.   [2] Memoirs, I, p. 268.

programme, but the aria, the duet, the quartet, the choral excerpt or the concerto still occupied the central positions right up to the end of the century.[1]

The musical literature of the 18th century has to be fine-combed in order to find references to the playing of an orchestra. The searching historian must read page after page about the singing of the vocalists and the playing of the violinist or the flautist, and then be truly grateful if he is thrown a word about the orchestra. There is so much that those authors could have told us about their orchestras; but they didn't. They were writing for the readers of their own time, and what they wrote about makes it very clear that it was the individual rather than the corporate performance that interested their public. The singing of a choir or the playing of an orchestra were to them small matters compared with the excellence of this singer's shake or the extent of that singer's compass.

What little can be gleaned about the 18th century orchestras and their playing has been scraped together and forms the basis and authority for what is written in these pages.

[1] For programmes, see Dörffel, Pohl, Jahn, Brenet, Cucuel, etc.

CHAPTER II

CONSTITUTION AND STRENGTH OF ORCHESTRAS

Enquiries regarding the constitution and strength of orchestras in the 18th century can best be answered by producing such contemporary records, lists of players and other information as are available.

An ample number of such records is to be found in the German musical literature of the period. Allowing for a certain amount of inaccuracy such as is not uncommon in 18th century books of this sort, the sum of the information they provide supplies quite satisfying answers to enquiries concerning the number of players to each part and the general strength of the orchestral bodies for which the German composers of the 18th century scored their works, and by which they were played. The records of French orchestras in the first half of the century are rather scanty, but of the principal orchestras in Paris during the second half of the century ample information is forthcoming. Similar records from Italian and English sources are, unfortunately, not so abundant, but those that are available make it fairly clear that composers in these countries were neither much better nor much worse off than their German contemporaries in respect of the orchestras for which they designed their music. That the German orchestras outnumber those of other countries is explained by the fact that nearly every one of the courts of the many German and Austrian states, large or small, and nearly all large households, royal, noble or ecclesiastical, had their own musical establishments, each capital or royal residence thus forming a separate centre of musical activity. This decentralisation caused a widespread cultivation of musical art, which in France and in England was centred largely in the two capitals. The musical centres in Italy were more numerous and more widely distributed than in France or in England, a condition which again tended towards decentralisation, but in the few remaining outlying centres in Spain, the Netherlands, Russia and the Scandinavian countries, musical activity flourished mostly within the shadow of their respective capital towns.

That we are able to recover so many and more detailed particulars about the German orchestras of the 18th century is probably due to the strong proclivity which prevailed amongst German musicians then, as now, to write about their art on the slightest pretext. Italian or English equivalents of such as Marpurg's *Historische-kritische Beyträge* (1754–57) and Forkel's *Musikalischer Almanach für Deutschland* (1782–84), two of a number of periodical publications peculiar to Germany from which so many of the ensuing statistics are drawn, do not exist. Written, no doubt, mainly to interest and enlighten music-lovers in their own times, these two books have served to supply historical records which are almost unique, and provide us with information which otherwise would probably have been irrecoverable. The French *Almanach* or *Calendrier* serves in the same way for the Paris orchestras of the second half of the century. Perhaps it is only due to a lack of thorough investigation that comparatively few particulars about Italian orchestras of the 18th century are available, and it may be that a systematic search in the archives of Italian churches and theatres might yet reveal much that is at present hidden and therefore unknown.

Orchestras in the 18th century had three main fields of activity, namely, the church, the theatre and the chamber or concert-room. They served for the rendering of the ritual of the church in the Mass, the anthem or motet, and both in and out of sacred buildings for the cantata and oratorio; in the theatre they took part in the performance of opera, ballet, masque and other dramatic representations; in the chamber or concert-room (for public concert-halls were few) they rendered concertos, symphonies, overtures, suites and all forms of instrumental music then current. The interest taken in the various forms of music in which an orchestra took part always differed to some extent in each country. The Italians were largely interested in church and theatre music, wherein the vocal and the instrumental medium are combined; the Germans took the leading part in the development of purely instrumental forms, in the symphony and concerto; the French were specially interested in opera and ballet; while the English, as always, eclectic in their artistic tastes, gave a welcome to all forms of musical work, especially when they came from abroad, and developed a particular love for oratorio.

Orchestra	Date	Violin (1st / 2nd)	Viola	'Cello	Bass	Flute	Oboe	Clarinet	Bassoon	Horn	Trumpet	Drums	Remarks	Source
Anhalt-Zerbst (Hochfürstliche Capelle)	1757	8	1	1	1		2		1					Marpurg, III, p. 130
Ansbach (Kammer und Hof-Musik)	1782	12	3	5	2	2	3	3	3	4	?	?		Forkel, 1782, p. 136
Arnstadt (Count Anton Günther)	1690	?	?	?	?		2		1		} 5		Twenty-one musicians altogether	Terry, Bach, p. 64
Bamberg (Fürstliche Hof-Kapelle)	1781	10	2	?	2	2	?		1	?			Number of 'cellos, oboes and horns is not stated	Nicolai, I, p. 129
Bayreuth (Court Orchestra)	1740												27 musicians	Fester, p. 125
Bayreuth (Court Orchestra)	1742	6		1	1	?	?		3				From a painting on a table	Fester, Hohenzollern-Jahrbuch, p. 150
Bentheim-Steinfurt (Court Orchestra)	1783	4 / 3	2	2	1			2	1	2			One violinist plays clarinet; bass player also plays bassoon	Cramer, I, p. 784
Berlin (King of Prussia)	1712	6 / 5	2	} 5			4		3		?			Kapelletat, 1712. Schneider, p. 54

Place	Date										Remarks	Reference
Berlin (King of Prussia)	1754	{12	4	4	2	4	3		2	?	Viola da gamba, theorbo, and 2 cembali	Marpurg, I, p. 76.
Berlin (King of Prussia)	1772	{12	4	5	2	4	4		2		Two harpsichords, harp, and trumpets and drums for fanfares	Burney (Present State), II, p. 96.
Berlin (King of Prussia)	1778	{12	4	4	3	4	4	2	2	?	Theorbo and harp. Two harpsichords	Anon, *Briefe zur Erinnerung*, I, p. 101
Berlin (King of Prussia)	1782	6 }7	4	4	3	4	3		2	?		Forkel, 1782, p. 146
Berlin (King of Prussia)	1787	{20	6	8	4	2	4	2	4	2	Three trombones. Harp	Anon., *Bemerkungen.*
Berlin (Döbbelin Theatrical Company)	1782	4 }4	2	1	?	}2			2	1	When flutes and oboes are required together, two more flautists are available	Forkel, 1782, p. 151
Prince Carl of Prussia	1754	{5	1	1	1	1	3	1	2			Marpurg, I, p. 156
Prince Henry of Prussia	1754	{4	1	1	1	1	1					Marpurg, I, p. 85
Prince Henry of Prussia	1782	{5	2	2	1	2			2			Forkel, 1782, p. 149
Crown Prince of Prussia	1782	{8	2	3	1	2	2	2	2			Forkel, 1782, p. 149

Orchestra	Date	Violin 1st 2nd	Viola	'Cello	Bass	Flute	Oboe	Clarinet	Bassoon	Horn	Trumpet	Drums	Remarks	Source
Bonn (Hof-musik) ..	1782	8 (+4)	4	2	}		2	}	2	4			Four *Accessisten*	Forkel, 1782, p. 129
Bonn (Hof-musik) ..	1783	9 (+2)	2	2	2	2	2	}	3	4	3	1	Two *Accessisten*	Cramer, I, p. 384
Breslau (Bishop) ..	1754	7	1	1	1	}	2		2	2				Marpurg, I, p. 446
Brunswick (Hof-musik) ..	1731	8	1	2	1	}	5		3	2				"7 Trompeter so bei der Musik" Kapelletat
Cassel .. (Hof-musik) ..	1782	5 / 6	1	2	2	2	2		2	2					Forkel, 1782, p. 139
Cassel .. (Hof-musik) ..	1783	7 / 7	2	2	2	2	2		3	2					Cramer, I, p. 146
Coblenz .. (Hof-musik) ..	1782	13	4	2	3	3	3	2	3	4	2	1		Forkel, 1782, p. 151
Dresden (King of Poland) ..	1697	6	?	?	?		6		3		3	1	Theorbo and six other instruments which are not specified	Mennicke, p. 272
Dresden (King of Poland) ..	1709	4	2	4	1	2	4		2		?	?	Also 1 *Haute-contre* and 1 *Taille*, probably viols. Two theorbos	Mennicke, p. 272
Dresden (King of Poland) ..	1719	7	5	5	5	2	5		3	2	?	?	One pantaleon, 2 theorbos	*Orchesteretat*, Mennicke, p. 273

Place	Date	Violins										Remarks	Authority
Dresden (King of Poland)	1731	} 6	3	4	2	3	4	3	2	?	?	Two harpsichords	Hofkalender, 1732
Dresden (King of Poland)	1734	} 12	4	5	2	3	3	?	2	?	?		Mennicke, p. 270
Dresden (King of Poland)	1754	8 | 7	4	3	3	2	5	5	2	?	?	Trumpets and drums for fanfares (see p. 42)	Rousseau, *Dictionnaire*, Pl. G, Fig. 1.
Dresden (King of Poland)	1756	} 16	4	4	2	3	5	4	2	?	?		Marpurg, II, p. 475
Dresden (King of Poland)	1782	} 17	4	3	4	3	5	4	3	?	?		Forkel, 1782, p. 143
Dresden (King of Poland)	1783	8 | 7	4	4	3	3	4	4	3	?	?		Cramer, I, p. 1236
Esterház (Prince Esterhazy)	1783	} 11	2	2	2	} 3		2	2	?	?	The violins included Haydn himself	Forkel, 1783, p. 100
Gotha (Herzogliche Hofcapelle)	1782	} 9	1	2	1	} 3		1	4	?	?	One 'cellist also plays oboe	Forkel, 1782, p. 140
Gotha (Herzogliche Hofcapelle)	1754	} 6	2	1	1	2	2	1	2	?	?	One lute	Marpurg, I, pp. 270, 560

Orchestra	Date	Violin 1st/2nd	Viola	'Cello	Bass	Flute	Oboe	Clarinet	Bassoon	Horn	Trumpet	Drums	Remarks	Source
Grosswardein (Bishop)	1765	34 musicians, including 4 vocalists											Twelve solo players, 9 servants in livery, a valet, a confectioner, 7 musicians and 4 vocalists	Dittersdorf, p. 144
Hamburg (Opera)	1738	} 8	3	2	2	5	4		5	4	4	1	Viola d'amore, Gamba, 2 piccolo, 2 zuffolo, traversa bassa, quart flöte, 2 cornetti, 2 oboe d'amore, Hautbois haute-contre, 2 chalumeau, 2 trombe di caccia	Kleefeld, I, p. 219
Hannover (Court Orchestra)	1782	21 musicians												Forkel, 1782, p. 135
Johannisburg (Prince-Bishop of Breslau)	1770	17 musicians											Eleven were salaried, the rest were household servants	Dittersdorf, p. 208
Kopenhagen (Court Orchestra)	1784	} 7	2	2	2	2	2		2	2	?	?	Harp	Forkel, 1784, p. 152
Leipzig (Concert-Gesellschaft)	1746	5 / 5	1 (+2)	2	2	} 3			3	2	(2	1)	One violinist also plays trumpet; 2 vocalists also play viola; 1 flautist also plays trumpet. Two horn players also play string instruments	Dörffel, p. 6
Leipzig (Concert-Gesellschaft)	1765	8	3	2	2	2	2		2	2	?	?		Gerber, *Lexikon*, art. Hiller
Leipzig (Gewandhaus)	1781	6	3	} 4		2	2		3	2	2	1		Dörffel, p. 22

Orchestra	Date											Remarks	Source
Leipzig (Bach)	1730	3	3	2	2	1	2	2	2	2	?	Partly amateurs. The bassoon was an apprentice	Terry, Bach's Orchestra, p. 9.
London (The King's Band)	1710 to 1755	From 24 to 26 musicians											Chrysander, from State records
London (Foundling Hospital) (Handel)	1759	12 (brace)		3	3	2	4	4	2	2	1		Rockstro, p. 259
London (Salomon Concerts)	1791	12 to 16 (brace)		4	3	4	2	?	2	2	1		Pohl, II, p. 121
Mannheim (Court Orchestra)	1720	12 (brace)		2	2	3	2	15 (brace)		?	?	Trumpets and drums available	Walter, p. 77
Mannheim (Court Orchestra)	1756	10 (brace)		4	4	2	2	2	4	12	2	Trumpets and drum corps: "Annoch 12 trompeter und 2 pauker"	Marpurg, II, p. 567
Mannheim (Court Orchestra)	1777	10 to 11 (brace)		4	4	4	2	2	2	?	?	Trumpets and drums available	Mozart's Letter, Nov. 4, 1777
Mannheim (Court Orchestra)	1782	18 (+5) (brace)		4	4	3	3 (+1)	3	4 (+2)	4	?	Accessisten (probationers): 5 violins, 1 clarinet, 2 horns	Forkel, 1782, p. 123
Mayence (Hof-musik)	1782	10 (brace)		2	2	1	3	2	1	2		Organ-blower and instrument maker	Forkel, 1782, p. 127

Orchestra	Date	Violin 1st / 2nd	Viola	'Cello	Bass	Flute	Oboe	Clarinet	Bassoon	Horn	Trumpet	Drums	Remarks	Source
Mecklenburg-Schwerin (Court Orchestra)	1757	} 7	2	3	1	3	2		2	2	4	?	Four of the players are "*virtuosen,*" the remainder are for "*accompagnement.*" One doubles bassoon and flute.	Marpurg, III, p. 339
Mecklenburg-Schwerin (Ludwigslust)	1782	21 musicians												Forkel, 1782, p. 142
Milan (Opera)	1770	14 14	6	2	6	2	} 4	2	2	4	?	?	Two flautists also play oboe	Leopold Mozart's letter, Dec. 15, 1770
Munich (The Elector's Orchestra)	1778	} 17	?	2	2	2	3	3	2	4	?	?		L. Mozart's letter, Sept. 10, 1778
Naples (San Carlo Opera)	1770	18 18	?	2	5	?	?		1	?	?	?		Burney, Present State (Italy), p. 365
Paris (Chapelle-Musique)	1708	} 6	3*	3	(1)	2	2		1					*Haute-contre, taille, quinte. Theorbo "Gros basson." Theorbo player doubles on double-bass	Grillet, II, p. 42.
Paris (Opéra)	1713	} 12	*	8		{ 8 hautbois, flûtes ou bassons						1	* Two quintes, 2 tailles, 3 haute-contres	Travenol et Durey de Noinville, I, p. 121

Place	Date												Remarks	Source
Paris (Opéra)	1751	}16	6	12*	?	}5	4	1	1	1	1		*Petit choer 4, grande choer 8. Clavecin	*Almanach*, 1752
Paris (Concert spirituel)	1751	}16	2	6	2	}5	3	2	1	1				*Almanach*, 1752
Paris (Fontainbleau)	1754	7 | 7	6				4	2	1				"les deux cors de chasse du duc de Villeroy"	Cucuel, *Études*, p.15
Paris (Opéra)	1754	}16	6	}12	2	}6	3	2	1	?			Basses include 2 viola da gamba	Marpurg, I, p. 194
Paris (Concert spirituel)	1754	}16	2	6	2	}5	3	?						Marpurg, I, p. 192
Paris (La Pouplinière)	1762	}5	1	(1)	1	1	2	1		2			Clavecin, 2 harps. Some players were double-handed	Cucuel, *Études*, p.14
Paris (Opéra)	1773	}22	5	9	6	}5	8	1	2	1	1			*Almanach*, 1774
Paris (Concert spirituel)	1773	13 | 11	4	10	4	2	3	2	4	2	2	1		*Almanach*, 1774
Paris (Comédie Française)	1782	6	2	4	1	2	2	2		1				*Almanach*, 1783
Paris (Comédie Italienne)	1782	6	2	3	2	}2	2	2						*Almanach*, 1783

ORCHESTRA	DATE	Violin 1st 2nd	Viola	'Cello	Bass	Flute	Oboe	Clarinet	Bassoon	Horn	Trumpet	Drums	REMARKS	SOURCE
Paris (Opéra)	1790	} 26	6	12	5	2	4	2	5	4	3	1	"Trombone et Trompettes" were the same players	Almanach, 1791
Paris (Concert spirituel)	1790	10 8	4	10	4	3	2	2	3	3	2	1	One trombone	Almanach, 1791
Paris (Théâtre de Monsieur)	1790	7 6	3	4	3	2	3	2	2	4	1	?	One trombone	Almanach, 1791
Padua (Church of San Antonio)	1770	} 8	4	4	4	4 wind instruments						}		Burney, Present State, p. 136
Poland (Count Branicki)	1754	4 4	1	1	1	2	2		2	2				Marpurg, I, p. 447
Pressburg (Cardinal)	1783	} 9	2	2	2	1	2	(2)	2	2	2	1	Clarinets doubled on string instruments. One viola was also copyist. Harp. Several players double-handed	Forkel, 1783, p. 99
Prague (Opera)	1787	3 3	2	2	2	?	?	?	?	?	?	?		Jahn, II, p. 300
Regensburg (Court Orchestra)	1783	} 12	2	2	2	2	2	2	2	4	4	1		Forkel, 1783, p. 102
Salzburg (Archbishop)	1757	} 10	2	3	2	} 3			4	2	10	2	Three trombones for Church music. Many players were double-handed	Marpurg, III, p. 183

Orchestra	Date	Total											Notes	Reference
Markgraf Friedr. Heinrich von Schwedt	1782	{ 6	2	2	2	2	2		3	2	3	·		Forkel, 1782, p. 150
Schwarzburg-Rudolstadt (Court Orchestra)	1757	{ 8	3	3	3	2	3		1	2	3	1	Several players double-handed	Marpurg, III, p. 77
Stuttgart (Court Orchestra and Opera)	1757	{ 15	?	4	4	3	3		?	4	?	?	Players divided into "Kammer" and "Hof" musicians	Marpurg, III, p. 65
Stuttgart (Court Orchestra and Opera)	1772	{ 18	6	3	3	2	4		2	3	?	?		Burney, Present State, I, p. 103
Stuttgart	1782	{ 13	6	3	3	2	3		2	2	?	?	Six violins, 2 cello, 1 bass, 1 flute and 1 bassoon are "Kammer-virtuosen"	Forkel, 1782, p. 132
Vienna (Hof-musik)	1721	{ 23	?	4	4	5	5		4	1	16	2	Gamba, lute, 2 cornetti, 4 trombones	Köchel, p. 21
Vienna (Hof-musik)	1730	{ 32							5	1	13	1	Gamba, lute, theorbo, 4 trombones	Küchelbecker
Vienna (Opera)	1781-3	6 | 6	4	3	3	2	2	2	2	4	2	1		Jahn, I, p. 631, II, p. 200
Vienna (Court Orchestra)	1782	{ 10	?	2	2	?	?	?	2	?	?	?	Three trombones for Church music	Forkel, 1782, p. 130
Weimar (Ducal Orchestra)	1700	{ 2	?	}1		?	?		1		5	1		Terry, Bach, p. 92
Weimar (Ducal Orchestra)	1714	{ 4	?	}1		?	?		2		7	1	The 4 violins include J. S. Bach as *Concertmeister*	Terry, Bach, p. 92

The 18th century saw some growth in the size and the constitution of the orchestra, and in the development of orchestration as a conscious part of the composer's equipment; it saw an increased advancement of instrumental technique, the gradual rejection of instruments which were unable to pull their weight in the growing body, and their replacement by those better fitted for the purpose. How, exactly, were these instrumental bodies constituted? And what was their strength? The first of these questions can be only partially answered by examining the scores and parts written in the 18th century, and the second only by reviewing lists of the personnel of orchestras derived from contemporary sources. The foregoing (pp. 18–27) is an attempt to assemble in tabular form what is known of the strength of 18th century orchestras. It is not claimed that it is complete, or that every possible source of information has been exhaustively drained, but it is sufficiently ample and representative enough to give an all-round view of the strength of the orchestras on which were played an immeasurably large quantity of music which has long since been neglected and almost completely forgotten, and on which were also played the more enduring works which still figure in our programmes. For the present purpose it has not been considered necessary to include in the lists all the players on keyboard-instruments, harps, lutes or other chordal instruments, or the vocalists who formed part of most musical establishments in the 18th century. The reader may be reminded that an "orchestra," when that word was used, generally included both vocalists and instrumentalists.[1]

It will be of some interest to analyse the figures in the foregoing tables, and to deduce from them the average strength and the balance of tone between the parts, first of all, in the string section of the orchestras. It was suggested earlier in this chapter that allowance should be made for a certain amount of probable inaccuracy, to which we may add some lack of precision, in these records of a musical past, which it should be remembered were largely written for present consumption, and not in particular for the benefit of future historians. Most of our authorities, for example, do not tell us how the violins were divided into firsts and seconds, and several lists fail to give any figures for the violas. It is possible that in such cases the violas were counted amongst

---

[1] English writers generally used the word "band" to distinguish the instrumental portion of a performing body.

the violins, or perhaps our informants didn't know, and left it at that. But, as viola parts are included in so many 18th century scores, it must be presumed that the instrument was represented in all but possibly the very smallest orchestras. Again, we are sometimes given only one figure for 'cellos and double-basses, and are left to guess in what proportion each of these instruments was employed. Some of our sources can supply no more information than lies in the bare statement that "21 musicians," for example, formed the personnel of a certain musical establishment. In such cases it is probable that the number given includes the *Kapellmeister*, organist, vocalists and possibly a copyist, as well as the string and wind players. Such want of precision makes any exact analysis impossible, but the averages of the available figures will no doubt provide a very fair estimate of the numbers of players to each part.

The average strength of the string parts in the orchestras concerned works out roughly as follows:

Six 1st violins, six 2nd violins, three violas, three 'cellos, two double-basses.

These figures, however, probably represent more than the average strength of the strings in 18th century orchestras, because the available data includes all the largest and most important orchestras of the period under survey, but does not include all the smaller and less important bodies. The well-furnished orchestras of the Prussian court at Berlin, Hasse's famous orchestra at Dresden, the opulent orchestra of the Milan opera with its 14 first and 14 second violins, the much-admired orchestra of the Elector at Mannheim, the orchestra at the San Carlo opera house at Naples which, according to Burney, had 18 first and 18 second violins, the orchestras at the Paris *Opera* and the *Concert spirituel*, the *Hofkapelle* at Vienna and Jommelli's excellent body of players at Stuttgart, these were the most famous and largest orchestras of the 18th century, each in their own period of bloom. Attention is naturally drawn to them on account of their importance, but their wealth in string instruments no more represents the average strength of the string section of 18th century orchestras as a whole than does the full strength of 100 players or more in one of our most prominent orchestras represent the average strength of English orchestras at the present time. These specially favoured bodies, among them, give an average of the string instruments approximately

B*

as follows:—9 to 10 — 9 to 10 — 5 — 4 — 4, which average is considerably raised by the exceptional figures given for the Milan and Naples opera houses.

If these nine famous orchestras are withdrawn from the lists, and the average is taken of those that remain, the resulting figures will give a much more true picture of the strength of most 18th century orchestras. The revised averages then work out approximately as follows: 4 — 4 — 2 — 2 — 2. These figures correspond exactly to those given by Marpurg in 1757 (the year after Mozart's birth) for the Archbishop's orchestra at Salzburg, and are only a little short in the strength of the violins (according to Forkel) of Haydn's orchestra at Esterház in 1783.

Even then, it should be remembered, the available data relate almost entirely to permanent orchestras, most of them of some repute and several of them under the direction of well-known musicians, and that their personnel was therefore considered to be a matter of sufficient interest to merit its being recorded in print.

The enormous number of sets of orchestral parts which are preserved in many musical libraries and collections point to the existence in the 18th century of a large number of small orchestras which enjoyed no particular repute. In theatres, pleasure gardens, private houses and in semi-public concert-rooms, smaller bodies of instrumentalists were obviously employed, and although records of their strength are not recoverable, it may safely be assumed that their players were few. If all such could be taken into account, it would probably be found that the average strength of the string players would be still further reduced, and that many 18th century composers' works were commonly played by a string group consisting of no more than two or three first, two or three second violins, and one each of the lower string instruments. Many old sets of parts which contain *no duplicate* string parts do rather suggest that many orchestras employed no more string players to each part than could read from one copy,—usually two, or at most three players to a violin part. The researches of the late Dr. Terry show that Bach, with the meagre resources of the Ducal orchestra at Weimar, with his total of 18 players (including wind instruments) at Cöthen, and a string group of 3 — 3 — 2 — 2 — 1 (partly amateurs) at Leipzig, was not much better or much worse off for string players than many others who made do with little skeleton chamber orchestras, sometimes composed of players who were by no means fully efficient.

The result of averaging the strength of the string players has therefore given results approximately as follows:—

Small orchestras: 2 or 3 — 2 or 3 — 1 — 1 — 1.
Medium orchestras: 4 — 4 — 2 — 2 — 2.
Large orchestras: 6 — 6 — 3 — 3 — 2 or 3.
Exceptional orchestras: 9 or 10 — 9 or 10 — 5 — 4 — 4.

Support for the above estimates will be found in the testimony of German 18th century musicians who have left us their views on how a well-balanced string orchestra should be constituted. Quantz's figures[1] are as follows:—

2 — 2 — 1 — 1 — 1   No wind
3 — 3 — 1 — 1 — 1   One bassoon ⎫
4 — 4 — 2 — 2 — 2   2 flutes, 2 oboes, 2 bassoons ⎬ Horns.
5 — 5 — 2 — 3 — 2   Ditto. ⎪
6 — 6 — 3 — 4 — 2   4 flutes, 4 oboes, 3 bassoons ⎭

In Koch's *Lexikon* (1802)[2] the figures are:—

4 — 4 — 2 — 2 — 2
5 — 5 — 3 — 3 — 2

Quantz's figures would apply to the period of Bach, while Koch's period covers that of Haydn and Mozart.

The division of the violins into firsts and seconds of equal strength has been made in these instances for the purpose of comparison with the previous figures; neither Quantz nor Koch gave other than the total number of violinists, but judging by the tables provided earlier, when any such division is shown, the general custom appears to have been to employ these instruments in two parts of equal strength rather than to adjust the balance in favour of the first violins. The layout of the string parts in 18th century scores, especially the duet-like partnership of the two violin parts, also supports the assumption that these two parts were generally played by bodies of equal strength,[3] even if not always by players of equal ability.

[1] *Versuch*, XVII, Sec. I, par. 16.   Compare the Berlin Orchestra of 1754 when Quantz was there.
[2] Art. *Besetzung*.
[3] See Bach's Memorandum (Leipzig, 1730) in which he asks for two or three first and two or three second violins (Terry, A Biography, p. 201; Bach's Orchestra, p. 7).

Allowing for inaccuracies and shortcomings in the available lists, and for any possible misrepresentation which the process of averaging may entail, the general conclusion cannot be far wrong, that, in the 18th century, orchestras were provided with a fairly adequately balanced body of string players of a strength which would be reckoned small in comparison with 19th century standards, and that towards the end of the century the number of players tended to increase.

With regard to the balance of the string parts compared with present-day standards, perhaps the most noticeable feature lies in the almost equal strength of the 'cellos and double-basses. But it should be remembered that for the greater part of the 18th century the 'cellos were treated orchestrally only as bass instruments. They supplied the general bass of the music in the 8-foot register, reinforced by the double-basses in the 16-foot register, and only when their capacity as melodists in the tenor or alto register began to be exploited towards the end of the century were they given any independence of movement. It may also be observed that, as will be shown later, the bass part in the 8-foot register was commonly doubled by one or more bassoons.

The proportion of violas to violins, rather lower than that which prevails in well-found orchestras of to-day, also finds a reflection in the nature of the parts allotted to those instruments in most 18th century scores. This will be discussed more fully in a subsequent chapter; for the present it will suffice to say that violas were only too often given parts to play which consisted either of the harmonic leavings of the top and bottom part, or were merely a duplication of the bass part an octave higher.

Before leaving the strings, a few features which emerge from the foregoing lists may be noticed. Traces of an earlier organisation, relics of the 17th century when the orchestra was yet in an early stage of its growth, are to be found, for example, in the occasional presence of the *viola da gamba* amongst the bass instruments. The five-part grouping of the strings in the Paris orchestras was likewise a relic of Lullian days, for the spirit of Lulli died hard in France. It is even possible that the *Hautes-contres*, the *Quintes* and the *Tailles* of the Paris strings in 1708 and 1713 may have been of the viol family rather than of the real violin type.

One or more of the keyboard or chordal instruments, which

provided a harmonic background for all orchestral music till late in the 18th century, must be taken for granted as part of the essential ingredients of all these orchestras.   The harpsichord, or two in the larger orchestras, the organ, lute, theorbo or harp, figured in all orchestras till the time came when, near the end of the century their services were gradually dispensed with as composers began to make their harmony self-contained and complete on the bowed-string and wind instruments.

The dominating wood-wind instruments in 18th century orchestras were the oboes and the bassoons.   Both already enjoyed a firm footing in that capacity towards the end of the 17th century.   A glance through the lists already provided will show that hardly any orchestra was without its oboes and bassoons; and even if the former are not specified, it is highly probable that either the omission was accidental or, more likely, that any flautists that are included in the lists were also oboe players. That this was the case is often suggested when only one figure is given for the number of players on both instruments.   Further evidence which supports this surmise will be produced when the question is considered from the point of view of the scores and parts.

The 18th century oboe was a simple affair, generally made of boxwood, with either two or three keys,[1] with a compass from middle C to D above the treble staff, including all semitones except the lowest C-sharp.   So it remained throughout the 18th century.   In larger orchestras, three, four or even more oboes were employed to play the two parts which were generally written.   The figures from Quantz already quoted (p. 31) show the number of oboes increasing proportionately with an increase in the number of string instruments.   It was only towards the end of the century that the use of oboes as *ripieno* instruments began to give way to the later custom of treating them as a pair of soloists, that is, one instrument to each part.   Some evidence, which will be produced later, strongly supports the view that one or more bassoons were commonly employed in playing the bass part in all 18th century orchestras, even though no part was written specifically for this instrument in the score.   The lists show that all orchestras had their bassoons, but written parts for these instruments were comparatively few till composers began to

---

[1] A three-keyed oboe is one with the D-sharp key provided in duplicate on either side of the instrument, so that it could be operated by the little finger of either hand.

release the bassoon from its duty of always playing the bass part, and gave it some measure of independence in the tenor register. This was only rather late in the 18th century. Quantz's list (p. 31) shows a bassoon already reinforcing the bass instruments in an orchestra of no more than nine string players; his group of 14 strings has two bassoons, and for 21 strings Quantz asks for three bassoons. The tables also show a very generous allowance of bassoons to the number of strings, and, on the whole, the figures agree very closely with Quantz's estimate. Three bassoons to about 20 strings were evidently not considered at all out of the way.

The bassoon began the century with an equipment of three keys, and finished it with the mechanical aid of from 6 to 8 keys. The compass was from low B flat, for rather more than two-and-a-half octaves upwards, of which range the two extremes were rarely used. Contrary to the usual custom of treating wind instruments always in pairs, the bassoons normally played the same part in unison.

The position of the flutes in 18th century orchestras was not quite so assured as that of the oboes. The larger orchestras apparently all had flutes, yet the scores and parts seem to point to the use of *either* flutes *or* oboes rather than both together. In the smaller orchestras the position seemed to be that, whereas oboes were regarded as indispensable, they could manage without flutes. There can be little doubt, however, that in places where it was impossible to afford two pairs of players, one pair played on either of the instruments, as was required. Examination of the old sets of parts will support this contention; so, when only flutes or only oboes are shown in the lists, it may be supposed with reasonable safety that one pair of players were able to take up either instrument. The earlier symphonies by Haydn and Mozart nearly all include oboe parts, and only occasionally, and then generally only for a single movement, are they replaced by one or two flutes. The lists of Marpurg and Forkel show only oboes in the orchestra at Esterház, and three players for both instruments in the Salzburg orchestra. The inference is, therefore, that one or more of the oboe players were also competent to play the flute when that instrument was required. The unusually large number of flutes in the Berlin orchestra may be explained by Frederick the Great's particular love of that instrument; on the other hand, in most orchestras which were able to provide players on both instruments, it is the oboes that usually outnumber the flutes.

The transverse flute began the 18th century with only one key, and a downward compass which did not exceed the low D. In the last quarter of the same century a few chromatic keys and two foot-keys were sometimes added to the flute, and the downward compass then reached middle C.

Whistle flutes[1] were still used in the earlier 18th century orchestras, and the parts labelled *flauto* or "flute" were certainly intended for those instruments. Parts intended for transverse flutes were always clearly distinguished by the use of such terms as *traverso, flauto traverso, traversière* or "German flute." The whistle-flutes gradually dropped out of use, and by the end of the century were no longer orchestral instruments.[2] As it was then no longer necessary to distinguish between the two types of flute, the various forms of the word "transverse" were dropped, and "flute" alone took their place.

Clarinet parts began to appear sporadically in orchestral scores and parts soon after the middle of the 18th century, and for about 20 or 30 years these instruments were occasionally used in place of oboes. No doubt, before they became common, the new instruments were played by oboe players. In Cramer's list of the orchestra at Bonn (p. 20), it will be seen that the clarinets and oboes are combined under one heading, probably indicating that both instruments were played by the same two players. With an increasing demand for clarinets, both in military bands and orchestras, the number of players would naturally increase, and in the course of time the new instrument would have its own specialists. Forkel's lists of 1782–3 show that clarinet players were by that time regularly employed in several German orchestras. Dittersdorf included a clarinet in the orchestra he organised for the Bishop at Grosswardein in 1765, and, according to Hiller, clarinet players were regularly employed in the Mannheim orchestra in 1767. Burney tells us that there were clarinets in the opera orchestra at Brussels in 1772, the first of which "served as a hautboy," and was "though a very good one, too sharp the whole night." In a letter written by Leopold Mozart in 1770 a specification of the orchestra at the opera in Milan includes two

---

[1] Recorder, common flute, or *flûte à bec.*

[2] "Because of its all too quiet tone and limited compass, this instrument has almost gone out of use" (Schubart, *c.* 1784–5, p. 209).

clarinets.   In Paris the new instruments were being used early in
the 'fifties, and early in the 'sixties we find parts for them in operas
produced in London.[1]   Further evidence of how this instrument
found its way into the orchestra, at first on the pretext that it was
a modified oboe, and how it eventually established itself as an
independent and valuable addition to the resources of orchestration, will be produced when the advent of the clarinet is considered through the medium of contemporary scores and parts
(p. 128).   The clarinets used in orchestras during the second half
of the 18th century were equipped with four or at most five keys,
and covered a range extending from the low (written) E to about
three octaves higher.

Looking through the lists given earlier in this chapter, one
cannot fail to observe the relatively large number of wood-wind
instruments employed in proportion to the number of strings.
The King of Prussia's orchestra, for example, according to the
lists of 1754, 1772 and 1782, shows the high proportion of one
wood-wind to every two string instruments.   The Dresden
figures of 1753, 1756 and 1782 give almost the same result, and
Forkel's figures for the Mannheim orchestra in 1782 are very
similar.   The proportion in Jommelli's Stuttgart orchestra is not
quite so high, yet, on the whole, it seems as if the German
orchestras rarely employed less than one wood-wind to every
three string players.   The Paris figures suggest that the com-
parative strength of the wood-wind in proportion to the strings
was not quite so high in France as in Germany.   The particulars
available for the Viennese and Italian orchestras are too incomplete, and probably too unreliable to make a fair comparison.

If we resort to the process of averaging the figures given in our
assorted collection of orchestral personnel, the result that
emerges is that, on the whole, 18th century orchestras employed
wood-wind to string players in the proportion of one to just a
little over three.   Quantz's ideal combinations (p. 31) are even
stronger in wood-wind power, and his larger orchestra of 21
strings and 11 wood-wind is quite in accordance with the Prussian
standard of his time.   Taken as a whole, it is clear that the
18th century strength in wood-wind tone was proportionately
greater than that of the late 19th century, in which a group of
eight wood-wind (one to each written part) generally had to

---

[1] Arne's *Artaxerxes* (1762) and J. C. Bach's *Orione* (1763).

contend with 30 or more string instruments.[1] The predomin-
ance of the double-reeds (oboes and bassoons) is a feature of the
18th century specifications that will not pass unobserved.

The great difference in the balance between the wood-wind and
strings according to 18th or to 19th century standards rests on the
fact that the earlier composers wrote for their wood-wind not
only as solo, but also as *ripieno* instruments.[2] In all 18th century
orchestration, of whatever period, any one instrument is liable to
be singled out to act as a soloist for a complete movement, or
sometimes a pair were similarly treated. This practice still
appears even in the more mature works of Haydn and Mozart,
and it never quite died out during the whole of the century. But
the earlier composers made a very clear distinction between a part
which was in the nature of a solo and one which was not. When
they were not using a wood-wind instrument as a soloist, they
expected the wood-wind to take their place on an equality with the
strings, to balance the string tone, to give, so to speak, blow for
blow, and to stand up to the string orchestra as its equal in power.
Handel, Bach and all their contemporaries, looked upon each
stave in the orchestral score as representing an equal amount of
tone-quantity; they didn't worry much about the "balance of
tone" in their orchestration, if, indeed, they ever thought about
such a thing. All parts were on an equal footing, and every
part was expected to make itself heard. The finer adjustments of
19th century orchestration were not necessary, nor did the circumstances which demanded such adjustments arise. Hence
the small string groups and the proportionately large wood-wind
groups of the 18th century orchestras. But, of course, to the
earlier 18th century composer, the string group was not small,
nor was the wood-wind group abnormally large. The two were
equally proportioned in tone-weight, and well suited for their
purpose. They treated the two groups as equals, and were not
concerned in making any particular effort to balance two groups
which balanced themselves automatically quite well.

As a sense for orchestral effect began to develop in the second
half of the century, and the functions of the string and wood-wind

---

[1] The earlier 19th century orchestras were balanced very much as those of the late
18th century. In 1813 Beethoven asked for not less than 4—4—?—2—2 strings to
the usual eight wood-wind (Thayer). Gassner's figures in 1844 are: 4—4—2—2—2.

[2] In a letter (Nov. 1, 1777) Leopold Mozart describes the performance at Salzburg
of a Mass by Michael Haydn in which six oboists took part, two as soloists and
four as ripienists.

instruments underwent gradual change, composers were faced with situations which demanded that some attention be given to the tonal balance between the two groups. The growing independence of the wood-wind parts gradually turned each type into a representative of a different sort of tone-quality. Their *quality*, not their *quantity* of tone was beginning to be valued and exploited; each wood-wind instrument tended to become one of a pair of soloists rather than just one voice in a choir of instruments. The *ripieno* character of the wood-wind parts declined; the mass-formation was gradually abandoned, till each instrument stood as one of a group of eight soloists. It was then that the flutes and clarinets came to be regarded *as* flutes and clarinets, and not as substitutes or alternatives to the dominating oboes. It was then that parts for two bassoons began to be commonly written, and then when that instrument became, not merely a common bass voice, but also a tenor soloist and melodist. By imperceptible degrees the wood-wind abandoned their communistic life in the orchestra and became individualists, and with that their numbers declined while the string orchestra continued to increase in bulk.

The mature orchestration of Haydn and Mozart both show the great change in the relative functions of wood-wind and strings in orchestration since the days when they wrote their first symphonies.[1] In the last three symphonies of Mozart and the last 12 of Haydn their composers do show some concern for the balancing of the wood-wind and string parts. But they were concerned with balancing 6 or 8 of the one type against 18 or 20 of the other; they didn't reckon that the same 6 or 8 wood-wind instruments would have to contend with some 30 or 40 string instruments, as they were often expected to do in the 19th century, and are still often asked to do at the present time.

Our orchestral lists show no signs that special players were provided in the 18th century for the few odd and less common wood-wind instruments which occasionally crop up in the full scores. But we may be quite sure that when parts for a pair of *oboi d'amore, oboi da caccia* or *cors anglais* were written, it was done with the knowledge that a pair of oboe players were available who had and could play these instruments. When Mozart wrote for a pair of basset-horns, either he would know that two of the clarinet players were able to produce these instruments, or

[1] Respectively, in 1759 and 1764.

perhaps he was assured that "die Herren David und Springer"[1] would be there to play the parts when his work was produced.

The octave flute or piccolo had no regular place in 18th century orchestras. The parts for *flauto piccolo* or *flautino*, which occur in some of the earlier scores, were intended for high-pitched whistle-flutes, i.e. small recorders or French flageolets.

The brass instruments came into the orchestra each by a different route: the trumpets via the army, the horns via the hunting field, and the trombones via the church.

Horns began to be used in cultured music very early in the 18th century, and before long had found a permanent place in most orchestras. From Bohemia, where it established itself in favour before the end of the 17th century, the *Waldhorn* quickly spread all over Germany and Austria, and Mattheson wrote of it already in 1713 that it was by then being used in church, theatre and concert music.[2] In France, except for a few tentative appearances in opera or ballet, it seems to have taken longer to establish itself as an orchestral instrument, and the dates usually given for the introduction of horns into the orchestras of the *Opéra* and the *Concert spirituel* are later than one would have expected in the country which gave birth to the *Cor de chasse*. When, just about the middle of the century, the horn began to be used orchestrally in France, it came back to the country of its origin in a new capacity. In 1750–51 the instrument was described as *Le nouveau cor de chasse*, or *Cor de chasse allemand*.[3] It was from the Bohemians that they learned in France how to use it artistically: *Les Allemands nous ont appris à employer les cors de chasse; ce sont eux qui nous ont montré combien ces instruments soutiennent et remplissent un orchestre.* So wrote Ancelet in 1757.[4] In this country the horns made a fairly early appearance, and are generally said to have made their English orchestral debut about the period 1715 to 1720. No reliable information

---

[1] "This instrument is as yet quite unknown here; it is said to be a sort of bass clarinet with a range of $3\frac{1}{2}$ octaves, a very beautiful and even tone throughout its whole compass, and to be playable in a very vocal manner. Messrs. David and Springer have recently played this instrument for the first time in several German courts and towns, and according to several accounts have not only overcome many difficulties, but have in every other respect played it in a most masterly manner." (Forkel, *Almanach*, 1784, p. 150) Vincent Springer, b. *circa* 1760, near Prague, pupil of Anton David, b. *circa* 1730 near Strassburg. (Gassner, *Lexikon*.)

[2] *Neu eröffnetes Orchester*, par. 7.

[3] Cucuel, *Études*, p. 26.

[4] *Observations*, pp. 32, 33.

has been found on which to base any estimate of when and how the horn found its way into Italian music, but Scarlatti's parts in some of his operas show that, at all events in the Neapolitan school, the horn was beginning to settle down at much the same time as it settled itself in this country.

Glancing down the column headed "horns" in the orchestral statistics given earlier in this chapter, it will be observed that there are very few blanks. Very few of those lists, however, date from before 1730.

In the earlier stages of their use in orchestras the horns were no doubt played by hunt servants who for the time being were pressed into the service of the musical establishment; but as the demand on their skill and musicianship increased, a professional and musically educated type of player would come into being, an indoor hornist who was unconcerned with hounds and hunting gear.

In the second half of the century, the horn, then no longer a mere offshoot of the chase, was firmly settled down in artistic musical circles, and long before the end of the century several distinguished players had taken worthy places amongst the *virtuosi* of their day.

Our statistics show that almost every orchestra, whether in church, theatre or chamber, had its pair of horn players, and that some of the larger establishments could produce two pairs. Nevertheless, it is only rarely that more than two parts were written for these instruments, and when that was done it was not so much for the purpose of increasing the amount of horn-tone, as was customary with *ripieno* oboes and bassoons, but rather because by crooking the horns in different keys a wider selection of open notes was made available.

The earlier horns were, no doubt, the plain *cor de chasse* or *Waldhorn* without crooks, but with increasing use for them in orchestras the demand for instruments that could be played in more than one key soon brought forth the orchestral horn with an outfit of crooks. The hand-horn with a tuning-slide, and the hand-horn with central sliding crooks both belong to the second half of the century, but while solo or *virtuoso* players made free use of the stopped sounds, the ordinary orchestral player was evidently not expected to be expert in the use of that device.

A casual perusal of our orchestral lists will give a very misleading impression of the position of trumpets and drums in 18th century orchestras. Looking down the column headed "trumpets and drums," we find either complete blanks, marks of interrogation, or else numbers of players, most of which are obviously far in excess of the needs of even the largest orchestra. The explanation is that trumpeters and drummers in the 18th century courts were not usually part of the household establishment, as were the musicians; they belonged to the military service; their duties were primarily of a military character, and their maintenance was not commonly charged to the household account. Every court of any pretension, in the life of which ceremony or display took any part, had its corps of trumpeters and drummers. Where the military and the musical establishments existed side by side, the former was called upon to supply the best and most musically educated of its members in order to provide the trumpets and drums in the orchestra of the latter. Thus, when we are informed that there were "7 trompeter so bei der Musik" at Brunswick in 1731, "annoch 12 trompeter und 2 pauken" at Mannheim in 1756, 16 trumpets and 2 drums in the *Hofmusik* at Vienna, or 5, 6 or 7 trumpets and a pair of drums at Weimar in the early years of the 18th century, we are not to suppose that such excessive numbers of trumpets habitually blew the heads off the rest of the orchestra. In such cases we are just being told the number of players in the corps of trumpeters attached to these courts, from which independent bodies the *Kapellmeister* were able to draw the three or four players they required for service in the orchestra, as occasion required.

Burney tells us how in the theatre of the Prussian court of Frederick the Great two bands of trumpets and kettledrums, placed one on each side of the house in the upper row of boxes, saluted Her Majesty on her entrance and at her departure from the theatre. To this he adds in a footnote: "This species of music, as it is the most ancient, so it seems to be that for which the northern inhabitants of Europe have, in spite of new fashions and refinements in music, the greatest passion. There is scarce a sovereign prince in Germany, who thinks he can dine comfortably, or with proper dignity, without a flourish of drums and trumpets." Old pictures and engravings frequently show trumpeters and drummers, mounted or on foot, taking part in processions or tournaments, playing at banquets or on other ceremonial and festive occasions.[1] We may be sure that

[1] See the pictures in Schünemann, *Trompeterfanfaren, Sonaten und Feldstücke.*

Frederick's *Kapellmeister* Graun could have trumpets in his orchestra whenever he wanted them. The anonymous writer who provided the figures for the Prussian orchestra in 1787 specified two trumpeters and a drummer; these, no doubt, indicate the players employed orchestrally on ordinary occasions.

Similarly, although neither Marpurg, Forkel nor Cramer include any trumpets or drums in the King of Poland's famous orchestra at Dresden, Rousseau tells us that in 1754 trumpets and drums were placed on a raised platform or gallery, one on each side of the orchestra pit; and from Zelter's *Autobiographie*[1] we learn that in Berlin: "the trumpets, 16 in number, were in two groups facing each other in the upper boxes next the stage, 8 trumpets and a pair of drums on each side. First the groups played alternately, and finally they joined forces and played together. When the king was seated the trumpets stopped playing, and an expectant silence ensued; the ear was cleansed by the sharp warlike sounds. Then the overture began, in which the trumpets and drums seldom or never took part."[2]

In commercial towns, such as Leipzig or Hamburg, it was the municipal trumpeters (*Stadt trompeter*) who were drawn on for occasional service in orchestras. As the restricting influence and priveleges of the old trumpeter's guilds died out and the elaborate and showy display of royal courts waned, civilian professional trumpeters would, no doubt, gradually replace the old court trumpeters towards the end of the 18th century.

Specific trumpet and drum parts rarely appear in the older concertos and symphonies, but became quite common before the close of the century. There is, however, some reason for supposing that these instruments were sometimes used, although parts specifically written for them are not found in the scores. In opera, oratorio and church music generally, both instruments were often used in big choral movements or when the words called for a martial or a spiritually exhalting echo in the musical setting.

Thus, we may suppose that, although our orchestral statistics

---

[1] See Ledebur, *Tonkünstler-Lexikon*, p. 660.

[2] At the court of the Danish King Christian IV at Kopenhagen early in the 17th century there were 15 trumpeters, of whom 6 were mounted. For the coronation celebrations, 17 German trumpeters were brought from Dresden, Koburg and Torgau (Hammerich). Fürstenau gives the following figures for the Dresden trumpet corps: 1699, one head trumpeter, 13 court trumpeters, 2 drummers; 1736, 13 court trumpeters, 2 drummers, 2 trumpet apprentices and one drum apprentice.

are so reticent on the subject, trumpets and drums would be employed in 18th century orchestras when the nature of the music demanded some special display of colour and brilliance, and when players were available, but that they were not treated as an indispensable part of the orchestra, except, of course, when special solo parts which formed an essential ingredient of the music were written for them.

The trumpets of the 18th century were just the simple un-mechanised instruments made in the form which still survives in the state or fanfare trumpets of to-day.   They were made in, or could be crooked in almost any key from 6-foot F down to low B-flat.   The parts of *zugtrompete* or *tromba da tirarsi* which appear in some of the older German church pieces must have been slide-trumpets[1] of some sort or else treble trombones.   Trombones had no place in the concert or chamber orchestras of the 18th century.   In Germany they were used in churches and in town bands, and they are found in the Vienna lists of 1721 and 1782, in the Salzburg and Berlin lists of 1757 and 1787 respectively, specifically for use in church music.   We can be sure that many a German *Kantor* would draw his trombonists from amongst the town musicians (*Stadtpfeifer*) for service in the church when special occasions required a full instrumental setting of the Mass, oratorio or cantata.   In 1784–5 Schubart wrote of the trombone in Germany as follows: "As it is so neglected nowadays, and is played only by wretched cornett-players, our musical leaders should make an effort to revive this sacred instrument. . . . Nevertheless, there are still some good trombone players, especially in Saxony and Bohemia.   Decidedly, the tone of the trombone is best suited for Religious, and not for profane music."[2]

There are traces of trombones in Italian and French church music, and, after a few earlier and sporadic appearances, they began gradually to find a place in opera orchestras towards the end of the century.   It seems as if these instruments were practically unknown in France during the first half of the century. Gossec wrote for trombones in his *Messe des Morts*, composed in 1760 and produced in 1762.   Not till about 1773–4 do they appear in the *Opéra* orchestra, played by Germans, but before the end of the century they were commonly used for French church music and grand opera.

Handel wrote a few trombone parts for his London oratorios,

[1] Possibly similar to the English "flat trumpet".
[2] *Aesthetik*, p. 203.

but it is hard to find many traces of these instruments in English 18th century music.[1] Burney tells of the difficulty which was experienced when trombone players were required for the Handel Commemoration Festival in 1784.[2]

A few other wind instruments which figure in the orchestral lists are relics of 17th century musical organisations. The medieval cornetts still lingered in ecclesiastical musical circles in Germany, and several obsolescent instruments occur in the list of the Hamburg orchestra of 1738. These, with the recorders, viols and lutes, really belonged to the musical past, and at the end of the 18th century were more or less forgotten, while the instruments which were to form the basis of 19th century orchestras were ever more and more consolidating their positions by proving their fitness for service in the still growing body.

A number of plans and directions designed to show how the players were placed in the music galleries, orchestra pits or concert platforms in the 18th century can be found. Their importance is emphasised by several contemporary German writers. Rousseau's plan of the Dresden orchestra in 1754 is well known,[3] and has often been reproduced. Quantz (1752), Petri (1782), Junker (1782) and Koch (1802) are amongst the older writers, Pohl, Dörffel and Kleefeld amongst the 19th century historians, who have contributed the data on which Mennicke and Schünemann, amongst more recent historians, have been at some pains to discover definite underlying principles on which to base their conclusions.

It is obvious that plans for distributing instrumentalists, and possibly vocalists as well, in places so variously constructed as the music galleries in churches, the orchestra pits in theatres and the differently proportioned platforms in concert rooms or music chambers, must differ very considerably according to the shape and size of the available accommodation in such buildings, and that local conditions would always have to be taken into consideration. Even allowing for all those varying conditions, it seems to be very difficult to discover any general uniformity in the plans and directions which the old authorities were so careful in laying down, except in a few respects on which there was not, and could

---

[1] See Handel's Horn and Trombone Parts (*The Musical Times*, Dec. 1939) by W. F. H. Blandford.

[2] An Account (Commemoration of Handel), p. 7.

[3] *Dictionnaire*, II, Pl. G, Fig. 1.

hardly be, any great divergence of opinion. All agree that the central point of the orchestra must be the *Kapellmeister* or director of the performance, and the instrument at which he officiates. Only in churches or in other buildings where choral voices were employed was a time-beater in control, and then not always. When both a time-beater and a keyboard-director were in charge, the two must obviously be in close touch with each other; both together formed the focal point of the performing body. As time-beaters were not considered either necessary or desirable in opera or concert performances, it was generally the keyboard-director around whom the performing members were grouped, and on whom their attention was centred. In·close touch with the keyboard-director was always placed the *Concertmeister* or violinist-leader, and at the elbow of the former was invariably situated the principal and leading exponent of the bass part, sometimes a 'cellist, sometimes a double-bass player, or possibly both, one at each side. Petri held that the leading player of the bass part should read from the music on the desk of the instrument played by the keyboard-director; that might be a figured bass part or a full score. That the *Concertmeister* (leader) should never be far from the rest of the first violins, that the brass and drums should be at the back of the platform or on either side of the orchestra pit, and that any soloists, vocal or instrumental, should be in front of the orchestra and close to the keyboard-director, are also matters on which authorities did not and would hardly be expected to differ.

Apart from the foregoing, it seems impossible to discover in the various arrangements offered any ordered plan for the disposal of the bulk of the performers on which all authorities were agreed. The relative positions of the first and second violins show no sign that the 19th century custom of placing the firsts to the left and the seconds to the right of the conductor was developing. Some schemes show them so arranged and others show their positions reversed. Some placed their first violins in front and the seconds behind them, while others reversed that order. The violas may be found placed almost anywhere, and the rank and file of the 'cellos and basses may be in a group in the centre, or on one side towards the back of the orchestra, or they may be scattered about in pairs on either side. More often than not, a 'cello and a bass play at the same desk from the same part.

If any ordered plan underlies all these varying arrangements.

it is very successfully concealed.   The disposal of the wood-wind players is as varied as that of the strings.   There seems to have been no generally accepted plan, except in so much that they are not usually placed together in a compact group, nor are they strung out in a straight line or in a semi-circle.   Petri, however, did place his oboes and bassoons close together, and gave two quite good reasons for so doing.   In the first place, he would keep them together because in orchestras which are unable to afford two pairs of players the same couple could conveniently move from the oboe desk to the bassoon desk and vice versa, as was necessary.   Even if such economy of man-power was not obligatory, the two pairs, said Petri, should be placed near one another because they so often play together in concert.

When a choir was employed in conjunction with an orchestra the arrangements for their seating again show divergent ideas on the subject.   Some would place the choir behind the orchestra, while others would have it in front of the instrumentalists.   Other plans are to have the choir on either or on both sides of the orchestra.   The number of voices in a choir relative to the number of players in an orchestra was, of course, much smaller in the 18th century than in the 19th or in the present century, and the vocal tone produced by a choir no larger, or possibly smaller, than the orchestra which accompanied it would not be dispro-portionate or overwhelming even if the voices were placed in front of the instrumentalists.[1]

In the 18th century, as in all other periods of musical history, there were occasional outcrops of performances by massed instrumentalists.   As mere curiosities these sporadic outbursts have some interest, but they lie outside the path of the growth of the orchestra, and should never be mistaken for anything but quite exceptional occurrences.   The following are instances of monster orchestras assembled for particular occasions:

1740.   *Rome,* an orchestra of about 200 players.

1784.   *London,* Handel Commemoration.   1st violins 48, 2nd violins 47, violas 26, 'cellos 21, basses 15, 1st oboes 13, 2nd oboes 13, bassoons 26, double bassoon (Mr. Ashley), trumpets 12, horns 12, trombones 6,[2] drums 3 pairs,

---

[1] At Mannheim in 1777 there were 24 singers to 20 violins and 12 basses (Mozart's letter, Nov. 4, 1777).

[2] "These performers played on other instruments when the sacbuts were not wanted" (Burney, An Account, p. 19).

double kettledrums, total orchestra **244**. Choir: soprano 53, countertenor 45, tenor 80, bass 84, total choir 262.

1786. *Leipzig*, "Messiah." 127 instrumentalists.

1786. *Berlin*, Handel festival.   Strings 38 — 39 — 18 — 23 — 15, 12 each of flutes and oboes, 10 bassoons, 8 horns, 6 trumpets, 4 trombones, 2 pairs of drums, total orchestra 167 (Hiller).

1789. *Berlin*, Dittersdorf's "Hiob."   Chorus and orchestra 230.

1799. *Dresden*, oratorio by Naumann.   100 instruments and 70 voices.

CHAPTER III

REPUTE, PERSONNEL AND STATUS

If we turn from orchestras in general to orchestras in particular, and try to recover from the scattered records of the past
something about the men who played in them, how they played,
under what conditions they worked, and in what repute they
stood, we need not expect to find much information about any
but the most prominent and best orchestras of their time, and
then always according to the estimates of their contemporaries.

Those on whose information and views we have to rely had
not yet cast a halo round the heads of those composers who
eventually proved to be the greatest of their century, nor did they
regard with reverential awe the places where these men lived
and worked. Bach at Leipzig, Mozart at Salzburg, and Haydn at
Esterház, were not at that time the high lights of German music.
Who, indeed, cared much about Bach's scrubby little orchestras
at Arnstadt, Weimar, Cöthen or Leipzig? and why should they?
There were dozens like them, no better or no worse. So when
Burney toured Germany in 1772 he did not even turn aside to
visit Salzburg or Esterház; but he made a point of going to
Dresden, Berlin, Mannheim and Stuttgart, to the shrines of
Hasse, Graun, Stamitz and Jommelli, where he could expect to
hear the best music, the best playing, and learn at first hand some-
thing about the "present state" of music in Germany.

Like Burney, let us now make a tour through the most important musical centres of Germany, France, Italy and England,
and see what we can learn, not of the "present state," but of the
past state of orchestras and orchestral playing in an age when
instrumental music was only beginning to assert its claim to be
regarded as something more than a mere adjunct to vocal music.

* * *

Already early in the 18th century, so Quantz assures us,[1] the
King of Poland's orchestra at Dresden enjoyed a reputation
which placed it head and shoulders above most others in Germany.

[1] Autob., Marpurg, *Beyträge*, I, p. 206.

This was apparently due to the excellent training of the *Concert-meister* Jean Baptiste Volumier[1] (1677–1728) who had introduced "a French style of performance." Volumier was succeeded in 1729 by Johann Georg Pisendel (1687–1755), who carried on the training in a "mixed style" (French-Italian), and brought the playing to such a pitch of perfection that Quantz declared he had never in all his travels heard any better. The period in which this body of players shone as a bright star in the orchestral firmament was when it was under the supreme charge of Johann Adolph Hasse (1699-1783), who was permanently appointed with the imposing title of *Königlich Polnischen und Kurfürstlich-Sächsischen Kapellmeister* in 1734. Hasse reigned until 1764 when, after many long absences in Italy, and probably as the result of political disturbances which included the Seven Years' War, he finally left Dresden and, with his equally famous wife Faustina, settled down in Vienna.[2]

How much the fame of the Dresden orchestra was due to Hasse and how much to Pisendel may well be a matter for speculation; but with such dual leadership as existed between *Kapellmeister* and *Concertmeister*, the one a busy composer and vocal specialist, frequently absent from his post, the other a conscientious and fully equipped violinist, always on the spot, one might hazard the guess that the real work was done by Pisendel while Hasse reaped the glory.[3] Pisendel died in 1755 and was succeeded by Francesco Maria Cattaneo.

Many prominent names appear in the records of the Dresden musicians. In a list of 1734 there were, in addition to Pisendel, Pierre Gabriel Buffardin (*c.* 1690–1768), a renowned flautist, and his still more famous pupil Johann Joachim Quantz (1697–1773). Quantz joined the orchestra in 1728 and left it in 1741, when he went to join the musical establishment of his royal pupil Frederick the Great at Potsdam. We learn from Fürstenau that already in 1711 two horn players, Johann Adalbert Fischer and Franz Adam Samm were engaged, and that a Pantaleonist[4] was included in

---

[1] On June 15, 1715, Volumier came to Cremona and ordered 10 violins from Antonio Stradivarius (Grillet).

[2] Hasse's period in Dresden corresponds roughly with the reign of his royal employer, Friedrich August II, King of Poland from 1733 to 1763.

[3] See Gerber, art. Pisendel.

[4] Invented by Pantaleon Hebenstreit at the end of the 17th century (Koch, *Lexikon*). A many-stringed instrument played on with two sticks like a dulcimer. Burney saw it in 1772, in ruins, at Binder's house. The strings were nearly all broken, and the Elector would not go to the expense of repairing them, nor could Binder afford to do so (Burney, Present State (Germany), II, p. 57).

1719. Marpurg's list of 1756 includes Pietro Grassi Florio (died *c.* 1795), the flautist who later settled in London and was there associated with the first efforts to provide the flute with an adequate key-system. Florio's colleagues were Wenzel Gottfried Dewerdeck and Franc. Joseph Götsel. The oboes included Antonio Besozzi (1707–81) and his son Carl (born *c.* 1738), two members of a renowned oboe-playing family, who were assisted by Franz Zienken, Christian Wopst and Johann Christian Taube. The four bassoonists were then Christian Friedrich Mattstedt, Johann Ritter, Samuel Fritsche and Franz Adolph Christlieb, and of the two horn-players, Carl Haudeck and Anton Hampel, the latter will be remembered as the initiator of a device which added considerably to the resources of that instrument. In 1756 the Pantaleonist was Christlieb Siegmund Binder (1724–89), and Buffardin's name appears amongst the pensioners.

Rousseau's opinion was that in numbers and the intelligence of the players the opera orchestra at Naples stood first in Europe, but that for the way they were arranged and for their excellent *ensemble* he awarded the palm to the Dresden players.[1] The value of his judgment, which in any case may be questioned, is somewhat discounted when we learn that his knowledge of the Dresden orchestra was acquired at second-hand, through Baron Grimm.

Burney visited Dresden in the course of his tour in 1772, and found the town and its musical institutions sadly scarred by the ravages of the Prussians. Of the old orchestra which had gained so many laurels in Hasse's time, the two Besozzis, Binder the former Pantaleonist, now organist, Neruda and Hunt the violinists, Götsel the flautist, the viola player Adam and one or two others were still there. Johann Gottlieb Naumann (1741–1801) was *Kapellmeister* after Hasse. Burney remarked that "it was from the dispersion of this celebrated band, at the beginning of the last war, that almost every great city of Europe, and London amongst the rest, acquired several exquisite and favourite performers."

Although he had long since retired from active work and was spending his last years in Venice, Hasse's name still appears as *Ober Kapellmeister* of the Dresden establishment in Forkel's list of 1782. The active *Kapellmeister* was then Naumann, as at the time of Burney's visit, and the *Concertmeister* was a Herr Babbi. Of the violinists, eight bore the same surnames as those

---

[1] *Dictionnaire*, art. *Orchestre*.

in Marpurg's list, and if two of these were the same old members, the others were probably sons or nephews of the old players. Only one viola player of Hasse's time, Joh. Gottfried Roth, was still playing in 1782; none of the old 'cello players remained, but Joh. Caspar Horn still played the double-bass. The new flautists were Adam, Derable and Schmidt, but of the five oboists, the names of both Besozzis and Zinke (Zienken?) still appeared in Forkel's list, although Antonio Besozzi had died in 1781. In Cramer's list of 1783, Antonio is replaced by Franz Besozzi. None of the old bassoon players remained, but Carl Christian Ritter, probably a son of old Joh. Ritter, was evidently true to the family instrument; his colleagues were Nessel, Zeissig and Braune. Carl Haudeck blew the horn as of old, but Anton Hampel is changed to Joseph Hampel in Forkel's list. Little more is heard of the Dresden orchestra in the 18th century. It had to wait for the advent of Carl Maria von Weber before its glories were revived in the third decade of the following century.

* * *

For some years before Frederick the Great's accession in 1740, according to Quantz,[1] the Crown Prince's orchestra had already gained a considerable reputation, and its playing had given the greatest satisfaction to many composers and visiting artists. When the new king transferred his musicians to the capital, several players of outstanding merit joined its ranks, and in the hands of its *Kapellmeister* Karl Heinrich Graun (1701–59), with his brother Johann Gottlieb Graun (1699–1771) as *Concertmeister*, the Berlin orchestra took its place as one of the best in Europe. Both of the Grauns had been in the service of the Crown Prince in Ruppin and Rheinsberg, Johann Gottlieb since 1732, and Karl Heinrich since 1735, and both remained in his service when Frederick became King of Prussia in 1740 and set up his musical establishment anew in Berlin. Quantz finally went to Berlin[2] in the year after Frederick's accession, and settled down there under conditions which were probably the most favourable ever granted to a wind-instrument player. His yearly salary for life was 2000 thaler (it was only 800 thaler at Dresden), he was given extra payment for his compositions,[3] 100 ducats

---

[1] Autob., Marpurg, I, p. 249.

[2] He had visited Berlin ever since 1728, specially in order to give the Crown Prince lessons in flute-playing.

[3] "He has composed more than 300 concertos for the use of his royal scholar" (Burney).

for every flute he provided, and was not required to play in the orchestra, nor was he under the orders of anyone but the king himself. But he was required to play with Frederick from 7 to 9 every evening, so perhaps, after all, he was not really overpaid.

Marpurg's list of the Berlin orchestra in 1754 includes several distinguished names. In addition to the two Grauns, there were the brother violinists Franz (1709–86) and Joseph Benda[1] (1724–1804), and Georg Czarth (1708–78). Johann Friedrich Agricola (1720–74) was *Hofcomponist*, Carl Philipp Emanuel Bach (1714–88) was *clavicembalist* until he went to Hamburg, not unwillingly, in 1767. The orchestral flautists were Johann Joseph Friedrich Lindner (*c.* 1730–90), Georg Wilhelm Kodowsky, both pupils of Quantz, Karl Neuff and Friedrich Wilhelm Riedt; the oboists were Karl August, Joachim Wilhelm Döbbert and Friedrich Wilhelm Pauli; Christian Friedrich Julius Dümmler, Samuel Kühlthau, Alexander Lange and Johann Christian Marks played the bassoons, and the horn players were named Joseph Ignaz Horzizky and Christian Mengis; the solitary gambist was Christian Ludwig Hesse.[2]

The best days of the Berlin orchestra were clearly round about the middle of the century, when the Grauns and the Bendas were in full vigour, their school of violin-playing in full bloom, and while their music still had some freshness about it. The establishment was ample, and the large opera-house, opened in 1742, made a good setting for performances on a lavish scale. No doubt Burney was not far wrong when he wrote: "At this time (1752) the whole band of vocal and instrumental performers was the most splendid in Europe." But the king was the dictator of musical taste; his musical policy was self-centred and narrow, and his influence was repressive. He would listen only to music which soon became out-moded, namely, the school of Hasse, Graun, Quantz and Agricola.

When Burney came to Berlin in 1772 both the Grauns were dead; Agricola was *Kapellmeister* and Franz Benda, then past his best, was *Concertmeister*. Philipp Em. Bach was no longer there; Lindner and Riedt still played the flute and some of the old players remained at their posts. Their playing did not quite come

---

[1] Franz had been in the service of the Crown Prince since 1733; Joseph came to Berlin in 1743.

[2] Son of Ernst Christian Hesse (1676–1762) one of the most distinguished of German players on the *viola da gamba* (Gassner, *Lexikon*).

up to Burney's expectations.   He had been at Mannheim, where he had heard the Elector's orchestra; no doubt it was the Mannheim playing that he was thinking of when he wrote "that the musicians of many parts of Europe have discovered and adopted certain refinements, in the manner of executing even old music, which are not yet received in the Berlin school, where *pianos* and *fortes* are but little attended to, and where each performer seems trying to surpass his neighbour, in nothing so much as loudness."

As the king became older his reactionary taste in music acted more and more as a bar to progress.   When Agricola died in 1774 and, after some hesitation, Johann Friedrich Reichardt (1752–1814) was appointed *Kapellmeister* in 1776, it was only on the understanding that the old repertoire should not be modernised. Nevertheless, Frederick insisted that the Berlin players should be well drilled, and Reichardt set about trying to infuse fresh life into a body which had lost much of its former excellence.   Two years before his appointment as *Kapellmeister*, Reichardt wrote of the Berlin orchestra, that "they play evenly and often with considerable vigour; because they have nearly all been trained in the school of our great Benda and Graun, they show an unusual unanimity of style.   But, to be quite candid, I consider that they are not sufficiently careful in observing the *fortes* and *pianos*."[1] In the anonymous booklet by "einem teutschen Biedermann," published in 1779, the situation is described as follows: "Everybody knows that the operas and orchestras at Dresden, Berlin and Stuttgart were the best in Germany when they were under the direction of Hasse, Graun and Jommelli.   The first and last of these have gone to pieces, and after Graun's death the Berlin establishment very nearly came to grief; but the present *Kapellmeister*, Herr Reichardt, with the support of Frederick the Great, has taken steps to revive it and put it in order again."[2]

With so many old players of long standing still in the orchestra, Reichardt's task would be no easy one.   Even as late as 1782, as Forkel's list shows, several of the players were the same as had figured in Marpurg's list of 1756.   Five of the violinists, including Joseph Benda, who was then nearly 60, had served since about the middle of the century; the newer violinists included three younger members of the Benda family.   Steffani, one of the old viola players, had been there since the days of K. H. Graun, but the 'cellists, led by Jean Pierre Duport (1741–1818) and the

[1] *Briefe eines aufmerksamen Reisenden.*   [2] "Biedermann," p. 46.

C

bass players were all of a younger generation. Of the wood-wind players, three flautists, Lindner, Neuff and Riedt, also an oboist, Döbbert, survived from the 'fifties, but the four old bassoon players had been replaced by two named Prinz and Damm. The horn players in 1782 were Selenka and Wenzel. That the traditions of the Graun-Benda school were still preserved during the 'eighties, is suggested by Cramer, who, writing in 1784, observed that the Berlin orchestra still retained a unity of style such as was rarely heard elsewhere; but he remarked that some of the once famous players were no longer there, and those that remained were old and played-out. Schubart's opinion was that "the Berlin school earned a great reputation, although its brilliance is now somewhat obscured"; but with the advent of Reichardt, things began to look up: "With this man, whom future generations will call great, began a new epoch in the music of Berlin."[1]

After Frederick's death in 1786 the restraint of the old regime was thrown off, and under Frederick William II, Reichardt would, no doubt, find greater freedom in carrying out a more progressive policy and in inaugurating reforms which were hardly possible as long as he was the servant of the old and conservative king.

Reichardt was one of the pioneers who abolished the keyboard-instrument in the orchestra, and was amongst the first to introduce baton-conducting. So, in his hands the Berlin orchestra was being prepared for the time when, in the following century, it was again destined to take a foremost place among German orchestras under the guidance of Spontini, just about the same time when the Dresden orchestra was being revivified under Weber.

Dittersdorf visited Berlin in 1788 and found the orchestra under Reichardt "incomparable." The players he picked out for special mention were: Duport the 'cellist, Georg Wenzel Ritter (1748–1808) the bassoon player,[2] Johann Palsa (1752–92) and Carl Thürschmidt (1753–97) the two horn players. These and several others " did what one could only expect masters of these various instruments to do." They were "quite worthy to be members of a Royal orchestra."[3]

Reichardt was succeeded in 1794 by Bernard Anselm Weber.

---

[1] *Aesthetik*, pp. 48, 60.
[2] "The finest bassoon player I ever heard" (Kelly, Reminiscences, p. 8).
[3] Autob., p. 274.

One wonders why the anomymous "Biedermann" did not mention the Elector's famous orchestra at Mannheim when he named "the best in Germany." His little book was published at Frankfurt in 1779, and Mannheim was not far away. First under Johann Wenzel Anton Stamitz (1717–57), and after his death under Christian Cannabich (1731–98), it seems to have deserved to rank quite equally with those at Dresden, Berlin and Stuttgart.

The great days of Mannheim's music began early in the 'forties under the rule of the Elector Karl Theodor[1] after the advent of Johann Stamitz. They lasted till well on in the 'eighties after Karl Theodor had become Elector of Bavaria, and the court and its musical establishment had been moved to Munich in 1778. Stamitz joined the orchestra in 1741 or 1742,[2] and became *Concertmeister* in 1745. He was followed by Cannabich, who remained in the Elector's service and eventually went with him to Munich.

Marpurg's list of the personnel of the Mannheim orchestra in 1756 bristles with well-known names. The *Kapellmeister* for the church music was Karl Grua (d. 1775); in the theatre Ignaz Holzbauer (1711–83) was in charge. Stamitz was *Concertmeister* for the concerts, and Alex. Toeschi for the church music. Cannabich, Karl Joseph Toeschi (1724–88), Johann Toeschi (d. 1800), Ignaz Fränzl (1736–1811) and Jacob Cramer (father) were amongst the first violins, and Wilhelm Cramer (son, 1745–99), who later became a prominent leader in London, was one of the second violins. The 'cellists included Anton Filtz (*c.* 1730–60), who together with Holzbauer, Stamitz, Cannabich, Joseph Toeschi and Fränzl, were already then, or became later, well known as composers. They were the mainstays of the so-called "Mannheim school." Johann Baptist Wendling (*c.* 1720–97) was first flute; the oboes included Alexander Le Brun[3] and the bassoon players were Heinrich Ritter and Anton Strasser. The horns were played by three members of the Zwini family, Joseph, Wenzel and Jacob, and by Matuska, all of whom were Bohemians.

When Burney came to Mannheim in 1772 the court was at Schwetzingen, near by, and there he found Holzbauer as *Kapellmeister*, Cannabich and Karl J. Toeschi as *Concertmeister*, the

---

[1] 1743.   [2] See Gradenwitz, p. 24.

[3] Probably the father of the famous oboist Ludwig August Le Brun, who was born at Mannheim. In Marpurg's list Alex. Le Brun is said to have come from Brussels.

former for Italian opera and the latter for French and German opera. Wendling still played the flute, and Jos. Toeschi, Fränzl, Wilhelm Cramer and Georg Czarth (from Berlin) were amongst the first violins. Burney found the orchestra all that he had expected it to be—"so deservedly celebrated throughout Europe" —and declared that "there are more solo players, and good composers in this, than perhaps in any other orchestra in Europe; it is an army of generals, equally fit to plan a battle, as to fight it." He admired their *crescendo* and *diminuendo*, which he rather rashly gave the Mannheimers the credit of having "invented," and noted that they had gradations of tone besides the mere alternation of loud and soft. The only fault he could find with the orchestra was the common one that the wind instruments were not in tune. The bassoons and oboes were too sharp at the beginning, "and continued growing sharper to the end of the opera."[1]

Several other contemporaries besides Burney have testified to the excellent playing of the Mannheim orchestra. Junker,[2] Reichardt[3] and Schubart gave it unstinted praise. The latter wrote, that "no orchestra in the world has ever played like the Mannheim orchestra," and waxed poetical over its *forte* like thunder, its *crescendo* like a cataract, its *diminuendo* like the burbling of a brook, and its *piano* like the rustle of spring.[4] Everybody admired the wonderful *crescendo*; Reichardt wrote in 1774 that "there is no *crescendo* like that of the Mannheimers."

Mozart went to Mannheim in 1777 and spent four months there. According to Jahn, it was at Mannheim that he first heard clarinets in an orchestra,[5] although it is almost certain that he had already heard them in London in 1764.[6] It was at Mannheim that he met *Kapellmeister* Holzbauer, whose music he greatly admired, and *Vicekapellmeister* Abt Vogler, of whom he had hardly a good word to say. It was at Mannheim that Mozart cemented his friendship with the Cannabichs and the Wendlings; it was there that he met Friedrich Ramm (1744—after 1808)[7] whom he provided with an oboe concerto, Franz Lang (b. 1751) the horn player, Ritter the bassoonist, and several others whose names occur so frequently in his letters. At Mannheim, Mozart

---

[1] Present State (Germany), I, pp. 94–97.   [2] *Zwanzig Componisten.*

[3] *Briefe eines aufmerksamen Reisenden.*   [4] Schubart, p. 84.

[5] The well-known extract from Mozart's letter of Dec. 3, 1778, has been often quoted: "Ah, if only we had clarinets too," etc.

[6] Abel's symphony, as copied by Mozart (K. 18), included clarinet parts.

[7] Ramm was appointed oboist in 1759.

planned his trip to Paris in 1778. He wrote of the orchestra there, that it was "excellent and very strong," and could "produce fine music," but that "as things are at present, you must write principally for the instruments, as you cannot imagine anything worse than the voices here."[1]

In a letter written in 1763,[2] Leopold Mozart paid high tribute to both the playing and the character of the Mannheim musicians. "The orchestra is undeniably the best in Europe. It consists altogether of people who are young and of good character, not drunkards, gamblers or dissolute fellows, so that both their behaviour and their playing are admirable." This, of course, was a reflection on the character of the Salzburg musicians, who were not remarkable for their moral virtues.[3] In another letter written in 1778,[4] however, Mozart's father qualified his praise: "The orchestra there (at Mannheim) is good and very powerful— but the interpretation is not in that true and delicate style that moves the hearer." In another letter in the same year,[5] the same writer gave a list of the Mannheim musicians who were going to join the Elector's court at Munich. Amongst them were Cannabich, the two Toeschis and Fränzl (violinists); Wendling and Georg Metzger (d. 1794) the flautists; Ramm, Ludwig August Le Brun[6] (1746–90) and Hieber the oboists; Hampel and Tausch sen. and jun., clarinet players; Ritter and Holzbauer, bassoonists; Franz Lang, Eck, Dimler and Martin Lang, jun., horn players.

The Mannheim orchestra evidently retained its excellence after it was moved to Munich. Friedrich Nicolai, who made a musical tour through Germany and Switzerland in 1781, was greatly impressed by the tone, the sureness and the unanimous bowing of the Mannheim players when he heard them at Munich. The playing surpassed all his expectations, and their *crescendo* and *diminuendo* had no equal in Germany. It was probably mainly by the playing of the string instruments that the Mannheim orchestra earned its great reputation, for the violinists were nearly all trained in the school of Stamitz and Cannabich, and thereby acquired a unity of method and style which was, no doubt, quite as distinctive as that of the Graun-Benda school in north Germany.

[1] Letter, Nov. 4, 1777.   [2] July 19, 1763.
[3] See Mozart's letter of July 9, 1778.   [4] April 6, 1778.
[5] Sept. 10, 1778.   [6] "A true magician on the oboe" (Schubart, p. 91).

In 1782, Holzbauer, then an old man of 71, and Vogler were still *Kapellmeister*; Cannabich and K. J. Toeschi were then, according to Forkel, called Directors of Instrumental Music, and Joh. Toeschi and Fränzl were *Concertmeister*. Of the violinists who were serving in the 'fifties, Danner, Ritter, Franz Wendling and Brunner still remained at their posts, and others named Wendling, Danner, Sepp, Ritter and Danzi, were no doubt sons of the older Mannheim musicians of the same names. Forkel gives the names of five *Accessisten*,[1] and of these, three, named Eck, Hampel and Strasser, again suggest that more of the younger generation were following the same profession as their fathers. Innocenz Danzi and Johann Fürst played the 'cello in 1782 as in 1756, but the three double-basses named in Forkel's list are all new. Wendling and Sartorius still played the flute, also Metzger, who was there at the time of Mozart's visit. The three oboists, Fr. Ramm, L. A. Le Brun and Joh. Wilh. Hieber are the same as those mentioned in Leopold Mozart's letter of 1778. Four clarinet players are named in the 1782 list—Michael Quallenberg, Hampel, Jacob Tausch and Franz Wilh. Tausch—the latter an *Accessist*. Of the bassoonists in 1782, Anton Strasser is the only one who was playing in 1756, and Georg Wenzel Ritter, who later joined the Berlin orchestra, Sebastian Holzbauer and Joseph Steidel made up a group of four players. Of the three horn players named Zwini who figured in Marpurg's list, only Joseph remained in 1782. He was then supported by Franz Lang, Mozart's friend, Georg Eck and Franz Anton Dimler. Two *Accessisten* on the horn were Franz Lang's younger brother Martin (b. 1755) and Joseph Dimler.

It is probable that, when it was at its best, the Mannheim orchestra was the finest in Germany, if not in Europe. That its example did much to improve the general standard of orchestral playing cannot be doubted, for many of the players and composers associated with it were enabled to travel about, and their influence seems to have spread far afield during a period when orchestral playing and orchestration were just beginning to awaken into active independent life. That Joh. Stamitz, during his sojourn in Paris, left his mark on French orchestral music cannot be denied. Wilhelm Cramer became one of the most prominent and influential of London's violinist-leaders, and the symphonies of the Mannheim composers Joh. Stamitz, Cannabich,

[1] Probationers.

Richter, Holzbauer, Toeschi, Fränzl, Filtz and Carl Stamitz were published in large numbers at Paris, Amsterdam and London, and were played far and wide before the mature works of Haydn and Mozart so completely took the wind out of their sails that they were never able to recover their places in the race which they at first led so vigorously and hopefully.

All honour, then, to the Mannheim orchestra, the "army of generals," the lusty string players, and even to the wood-wind players, although they did play rather out of tune on their imperfect boxwood instruments.

*   *   *

The glories of the Duke of Würtemberg's musical establishment at Stuttgart began in 1753 when Niccolo Jommelli (1714–74) came there to take charge. According to Schubart: "Under Jommelli the Würtemberg musical establishment became one of the best in the world."[1] We have learned from the anonymous "Biedermann" that this orchestra shared with Dresden and Berlin the distinction of being the best in Germany, but that now (in 1779) the period of blooming was over. Burney tells much the same story: "though the operas, and the musical establishment of this prince, used, during the seven years'[2] direction of Jommelli, to be the best and most splendid in Germany, they are now (1772) but the shadow of what they were."[3]

Marpurg's list of the orchestra at Stuttgart in 1757 should represent it at its best, after having been for four years under Jommelli. The *Concertmeister* was then Pasqualino Bini (*c.* 1720–68), a pupil of Tartini. From 1762 to 1773 Antonio Lolli (*c.* 1730–1802), a showy violinist of whom it was said that he could not play in time, occupied the same position. The principal flute in 1757 was Daube; Pla[4] (Plas, Plats) led the oboes, assisted by Commerell and Hetsch, sen., and the leading horn player was Herr Sporni, who was aided by Midlar, Schade and Zoebel. At that time eleven of the violinists, four 'cellists, one double-bass player and the leading flautist, oboe and horn players were distinguished as *Kammermusiker*, the remainder of the orchestra being only *Hofmusiker*.

When Burney came to Ludwigsburg in 1772 he found Antonio

[1] Schubart, p. 94.   [2] Jommelli was there for over 15 years.
[3] Present State (Germany), I, p. 100.
[4] One of two brothers, Spaniards, of whom Schubart wrote: "If Castor and Pollux had played the oboe, inspired by the God who begat them, they could hardly have played better than these two brothers" (p. 97).

Boroni (1738–92) in charge as first *Kapellmeister*; Lolli was still *Concertmeister*, and Curz and Baglioni were amongst the violins. He also mentions the four oboists, Alrich, Hetsch, Blesner and Commerell; two flautists, Joh. Wilh. Fried. Steinhardt "a very good one," and Augustinelli; two bassoonists, Andreas Gottlob Schwarz (1743–1804), "an admirable one," and Bart.

In 1782 Boroni was still *Kapellmeister*, and the *Concertmeister* was Pietro Martinez. The violinists of that date included the two mentioned by Burney. Steinhardt the flautist still figured in the 1782 list, although he had gone to join the court orchestra at Weimar in 1776. Of the four oboists named by Burney, Christoph Hetsch, Luigi Blesner and Adam Friedrich Commerell remained in service in 1782, as also the two bassoon players Schwarz and Bart. The two horn players at that time were Strohm and Greube, jun. As at Mannheim, the Stuttgart players specialised in *crescendo* and *diminuendo* effects, and claims have been made of behalf of both of these orchestras that they were the first to make use of these devices.

*   *   *

A glance through the statistics provided in Chapter II will give some idea of the number of orchestras maintained by the ruling sovereigns and princes in Germany during the 18th century. To these must be added probably quite as many again which are omitted only because particulars of their strength and personnel are not to hand. The musical establishments at Brunswick, Cassel, Mayence, Munich, Coblenz and Gotha, to name only a few, ranked second only to those at Dresden, Berlin, Stuttgart and Mannheim, and were amply provided with personnel which in many cases included musicians of high standing. Most of them experienced the same sort of ups and downs, which varied according to the political situations, the taste and material fortunes of their respective rulers, and the artistic capabilities of their musical directors.

The music at Salzburg quite naturally attracts our attention because there was the home of the Mozarts, just as does Esterház on account of its association with Haydn. In 1757, the year after Mozart's birth, the Archbishop employed close on 100 musicians at Salzburg, of whom 35 were singers. The instrumentalists included 10 trumpeters and two drummers, three organists and three trombone players, as well as the usual assortment of string and wood-wind players, and an attendant staff of three organ-blowers, two instrument repairers, and, no doubt, one or two copyists. The *Kapellmeister* in 1757 was Johann Ernst Eberlin (1702–62), and Joseph Lolli (d. 1778) was *Vicekapellmeister*. Of the orchestral players named in Marpurg's list,[1] none appear to have been or to have become particularly distinguished, excepting of course, Leopold Mozart, who became very well known as the author of the standard German violin school *Versuch einer gründlichen Violinschule* (1756), a book which for about half a century ranked equally with Quantz's *Versuch einer Anweisung die Flöte traversiere zu speilen* (1752) and C. P. E. Bach's *Versuch über die wahre Art das Klavier zu spielen* (1753, 1762).

An unusually large proportion of the Archbishop's players were double-handed, and a few carried their versatility so far as to play on three or four instruments. Thus, a violinist named Franz Schwarzmann could also play the bassoon, oboe, flute and horn, and the trombone expert, Herr Thomas Oschlatt, could acquit himself equally well on the violin, 'cello and horn. Six of the trumpeters also played the violin, and two of the violinists could take a turn at the horn.[2]

Michael Haydn, Joseph Haydn's younger brother, joined the Salzburg establishment in 1762 as *Concertmeister* after Eberlin's death, when Lolli was promoted to be *Kapellmeister* and Leopold Mozart became *Vicekappellmeister*.[3]

Burney did not visit Salzburg on his way from Munich to Vienna in 1772, although it would not have taken him far out of his way. Probably this was because he had learned on "good authority" that the Archbishop's band was "more remarkable for coarseness and noise, than delicacy and high-finishing." Mozart himself had no great opinion of the Salzburg musicians: "That is one of my chief reasons for detesting Salzburg—these coarse, slovenly, dissolute court musicians. . . . Ah, if only the orchestra were organised as they are at Mannheim. Indeed I would like you to see the discipline which prevails there and the authority which Cannabich wields."[4]

Most important at Salzburg was the church music. All the

---

[1] Jahn surmised that this list was supplied to Marpurg by Leopold Mozart.

[2] Old tutors for brass instruments often recommend students to learn to play a string instrument for the good of their musicianship.

[3] Jahn, I, p. 237.

[4] Letter, July 9, 1778. Kelly (I, p. 276) found the orchestra "numerous and excellent "

C*

leading musicians there—Eberlin, Leopold Mozart and Michael Haydn—were industrious composers of Masses and Oratorios. The music at the *Domkirche* was elaborate and showy. There were one large and four small organs, around which were grouped the singers and instrumentalists, including two corps of trumpets and drums. Trombones supported the choral voices;[1] oboes and flutes were seldom used in the church, and horns not at all. Schubart remarked that "the Salzburgers shine especially on the wind instruments. There one finds most excellent trumpeters and horn players."[2]

In the German towns where there was no court music the people themselves had to organise and support such orchestras as they could manage to maintain. The great days of Hamburg's music were late in the 17th and early in the 18th century, when Keiser, Telemann and Handel gave distinction to the opera established there by artistically minded citizens.[3] This languished in the 'thirties, and although Hamburg's music gained much by the presence there of C. P. E. Bach from 1767, Burney found in 1772 that he had come, as Bach told him, "fifty years too late." Nevertheless, Hamburg must have preserved some of its former reputation even late in the 18th century, for, according to Schubart, writing about 1784: "Although not very large, the theatre orchestra at Hamburg is one of the best in Germany; so correct is their playing that *Concertmeister* go there in order to learn how an orchestra should be led."[4]

Musical societies organised by the students and citizens supplied Leipzig with its corporate music in the early part of the 18th century. Out of these grew a larger concert-giving society on a subscription basis early in the 'forties at the "Three Swans" inn.[5] After some interruption during the Seven Years' War, these concerts were revived under Johann Adam Hiller (1728–1804), with Johann Georg Häser (1729–1809) as leader, and an orchestra of professional players, university students, town musicians (*Stadtpfeifer*) and amateurs, a mixture which, according to Gerber, was equal in quality to a good court orchestra.[6,7]

An important landmark in the story of Leipzig's music-making

[1] Marpurg, III, p. 195: "Endlich gebraucht man zum Chor 3 posaunisten."
[2] Schubart, p. 100.   [3] Kleefeld.
[4] Schubart, p. 109.   [5] See Dörffel's *Zeitschrift* (1884).
[6] Compare Bach's instrumental forces at Leipzig in Terry's *Bach's Orchestra*.
[7] Reichardt's account of a visit in 1771 to the "Grosse Concert" in his *Briefe eines aufmerksamen Reisenden* is interesting.

was the opening in 1781 of the *Gewandhaus*,[1] a public concert hall seating well over 500 people. Still under Hiller, the orchestra which flourished there, and which was directed after Hiller's departure from Leipzig in 1785 by Joh. Gottfried Schlicht, remained more or less a homely affair without much more than a local reputation until it began to develop early in the 19th century and burst into full bloom in the time of Mendelssohn.

Burney was at Leipzig in 1772, but did not hear the *Grosse Concert* at the "Three Swans." He did hear one of Hiller's *Singspiele* rehearsed at the theatre, and was not at all impressed with the quality of either the singing or the playing, nor with Hiller's ability as a director: "The instrumental parts went ill; but this was the first rehearsal, they might have been disciplined into good order, if M. Hiller had chosen to bounce and play the tyrant a little; for it is a melancholy reflection to make, that few composers are well treated by an orchestra, till they have first used the performers roughly, and made themselves formidable."[2] Mozart gave a concert in the *Gewandhaus* in 1789 which was poorly attended. Rochlitz tells a story of the rehearsal for this concert; how Mozart saw that the players were rather old and sleepy, and decided that they needed waking up. When they dragged the *tempo* of an *Allegro* in his symphony, he called for more and more speed, and in urging them on stamped his foot so violently that his shoe lace broke. To this Jahn added the information that a viola player was so impressed that he marked the place in his part where Mozart's shoe lace had snapped.

By no means an unimportant part taken by Leipzig in the cultivation and dissemination of orchestral music was due to the presence there of the publishing firm of Breitkopf. Soon after the mid-century Breitkopf had large stocks of MS. and printed parts of orchestral and other works for sale. His thematic catalogues compiled in the 'sixties and 'seventies have been of some value in helping to identify symphonies of that period of which the authorship was uncertain or unknown.

* * *

Music was cultivated in Vienna at the imperial court, in the churches and theatres, in the courts of the princes and nobility of the district around the city, and in the houses of its well-to-do inhabitants. Notwithstanding its importance as a musical

---

[1] For a full account, see Dörffel.   [2] Present State (Germany), II, p. 76.

centre, and the presence there from time to time of some of the most distinguished composers and executants, the musical records of Vienna provide only rather sparing information regarding its orchestras in the 18th century.

Of the brilliant period up to about 1740, when the imperial musical establishment numbered from about 100 to 130 vocalists and instrumentalists, engaged largely in the service of the church and for the performance of opera, oratorio and various court functions, it is difficult to glean any particulars of the instrumental side of their work. Fux, Caldara and Conti were then the court composers, the first two serving also as *Kapellmeister*. Wagenseil links that older generation with the later Viennese period of Haydn and Mozart. The court *Kapellmeister* Reutter, in whose period of office, from 1751 to 1772, the opera was handed over to the administration of the city, saw the musical establishment of the court fall to about 20 musicians, after which it revived considerably under Florian Leopold Gassmann (1729–74) from 1772, Joseph Bonno (1710–88) from 1774, and finally, under Salieri in 1788.

Burney tells us that in 1772 there was no longer any serious opera in Vienna, but that in the German theatre "the orchestra has a very numerous band, and the pieces which were played for the overture and act-tunes were very well performed, and had an admirable effect; they were composed by Haydn, Hoffmann and Vanhall." In the French theatre also he found the orchestra "full and striking as that of the other theatre, and the pieces played were admirable." In the cathedral of St. Stephen, Burney heard a Mass by Reutter, the former *Kapellmeister*, sung and played under the direction of Gassmann who was then court *Kapellmeister*. The music was "without taste or invention," and "as there was a numerous band, great noise and little meaning characterised the whole performance." Of the instrumentalists he met, Burney mentions Venturini, "an hautbois player of the first class," and La Motte,[1] "a Flamand, the best solo player and sightman, upon the violin, at Vienna."

Nor do we learn much about the Viennese orchestras from Mozart, who spent most of his time there after finally leaving Salzburg. He threw us one word in a letter describing how he found it advisable to direct personally a performance of his "Entführung" from the piano because he thought the players

[1] Franz Lamotte, *c.* 1751–81.

were getting a bit sleepy.   Like Mozart, Dittersdorf told us a lot
about the musical life of Vienna, but neglected to leave any
criticism of the orchestras there, which he would have been so
well qualified to do.

After drawing so many blanks it is refreshing to discover an
interesting and intelligent comparison of the playing of the
Berlin and Vienna orchestras written by Fr. Nicolai in 1781.[1]
Freely translated, this runs as follows: "I found that the difference between the playing of the Berlin and the Vienna orchestra
was much less than I had anticipated.   It was particularly in the
rendering of the Viennese symphonies that I had expected the
difference would be most marked, and I was surprised to find how
little it was.   In Vienna I heard symphonies by Haydn and
Vanhall played much as I had heard them in Berlin.   The
greatest difference was in the bowing, but even this was not so
pronounced as I had thought it would be.   It was most noticeable
where short and forcible bowing was required, such as demand a
particular style of playing in Haydn's works, and where short,
crisp notes occur in succession.   The Viennese orchestra played
such passages with a unanimity and precision such as is not yet
practised by the Berlin players, nor probably in any large orchestra,
even though several of the individual players are familiar
with this style of bowing.   On the other hand, passages demanding long sustained bows are not, on the whole, so well played in
Vienna as in Berlin; I have noticed this in the rendering of both
light and sacred music in Vienna.   This is caused by the generally
lighter bowing of the Viennese players.   A more subtle and still
more marked difference between the Berlin and the Vienna
playing may be observed in their rendering of *Andante* movements.   Even though such movements are played equally
correctly and in the same *tempo* by both orchestras, the Viennese
manage to give them a lighter touch.   Whoever has heard an
Andante or an *Adagio* written in the style of Hasse played in
Dresden and in Berlin will understand what I mean.   In Dresden
the playing is more springy than in Berlin.   In Vienna the tread
is lighter than in Dresden.   Skipping (*hüpfend*) is not exactly the
right word to use, and might give an impression which I do not
mean to convey.   The French expression *lestement* (nimbly) is
perhaps the nearest to my meaning.   On the other hand, in the
theatre I heard, played between the acts, a piece in a sort of

[1] IV, p. 541.

Grave movement, which, if I am not mistaken, was composed in Hamburg. Here, again, the difference between the Berlin and the Vienna playing was quite pronounced. The dotted notes in a *Grave* movement are played in Berlin in a more sustained manner, and with a more extended bow, than in Vienna, and thereby produce a rather different, and, in my opinion, a better effect. I have often noticed this in the playing of the more pathetic moments in sacred music as it is rendered in Vienna." In short, the Berliners were stolid and worthy, albeit a trifle stodgy, while the Viennese were a bit lighthearted, but nevertheless pleasantly attractive. Forkel gave a list of the *Hof-und-Kammermusik* players at Vienna in 1782, which, however, appears to be incomplete. The office of *Generaldirector*, an administrative non-musical official, was then filled by Johann Wenzel Graf von Spork. Bonno was still *Kapellmeister* and Wagenseil still figured in the list as court composer.[1] No *Concertmeister* is mentioned, but Lamotte, named by Burney in 1772, was amongst the violinists. No viola players, nor any flautists, oboists or horn players are named, but Forkel gave the names of three trombone players, and the two bassoonists named Phil. Friederich and Michael Anton Steiner.

The private orchestras of the Austrian or Hungarian nobility who, with their musicians, often spent the winter in Vienna, must be counted as part of the musical life of that city.[2] Of the musical establishments of Hildburghaussen, Schwarzenburg, Liechtenstein, Lobkowitz, Kinsky, Grassalkowitz and Esterhazy, the last has a special interest, not because of its outstanding merit as a performing body, but because it was the medium through which the greater part of the output of its *Kapellmeister* Joseph Haydn was brought to life.

In 1783 the *Fürstlich Esterhazische Kapelle zu Esterház in Ungarn* was under its *Direktor und Kapellmeister* Joseph Haydn, who was evidently his own *Concertmeister*, for Forkel adds that Haydn "spielt zugleich die erste violine." Of the 16 string players, only three can be picked out as having achieved any distinction, namely, the two Italian violinists Luigi Tomasini (1741–1808) and Nicoletto Mestrino (1748–90), and the leading 'cellist Anton Kraft (1752–1820). The others are not much more than names, some few of which have crept into books only

---

[1] According to Grove, Wagenseil died in 1777.
[2] See Hanslick, Chap. II.

because they happen to have been associated with Haydn.[1] No doubt the two oboists, Schaudich and Mayer, also played the flute, as they would have to do in certain movements of the many small symphonies which Haydn wrote for the orchestra at Esterház or Eisenstadt. Haydn's horn players in 1783 were Rupp and Mackoviez, and his pair of bassoons were played by Peczivall and Stainer. No doubt a pair of trumpeters and a drummer would be available when they were wanted.

In associating this orchestra with Haydn's works, it should be remembered that it was not for the smaller resources at Esterház that the composer planned his Paris and his London symphonies, nor "The Creation" and "The Seasons."

Another very similar court orchestra not very far from Vienna was that of the Cardinal Prince Bathiany at Pressburg. Here the offices of *Kapellmeister* and *Concertmeister* were evidently combined in the person of Joseph Zistler. The only notable names in 1783 were those of the leading 'cello player Franz Xaver Hammer, Johann Sperger the double-bass virtuoso, Johann and Philipp Teimer, two of three brothers who won some renown as oboists, Karl Franz (1738–1802) and Anton Böck (b. 1757), both well-known horn players.[2] As in many other 18th century orchestras, several of the players at Pressburg were double-handed; thus, the violinist Franz Czerwenka could be turned on to play the bassoon, and Anton Nikusch combined the duties of violinist and flautist. Another violinist, Michael Bum, also acted as second clarinettist, and the leading viola player, Theodor Lotz, who won musical-dictionary-fame as an improver of the bassethorn, was likewise the leading clarinet player when that instrument was required.

These two, at Pressburg and Esterház, were typical of many of the smaller court orchestras of South Germany, Austria, Hungary and Bohemia in the second half of the 18th century.

* * *

The Royal orchestra in Paris (*Musique du Roi*), like the King's Band in London, and unlike the court orchestras in the German capitals, was not the dominating influence in the development of French orchestras during the 18th century.[3] The centre of

---

[1] "His band was formed of great professors" (Kelly, I, p. 218).

[2] Towards the end of the century the brothers Ignaz and Anton Böck toured Europe extensively as virtuoso horn duettists (Gassner, *Lexikon*).

[3] "Whoever enters the King's service, is forgotten in Paris" (Mozart, Letter, July 3, 1778).

activity, and the scene of progress lay in the leading opera and concert orchestras, namely, those of the *Opéra* (*Académie Royale de Musique*) and the *Concert spirituel*. These two bodies, although sharing many of the same players, were rather differently constituted and served different purposes. The one is closely wrapped up with the history of French grand opera, and the other with that of French symphonic music. Nevertheless, some share in the proceedings must be allowed to the smaller orchestras of the Paris theatres where, at various times during the century, Italian and lighter opera were produced, such as—the *Opéra Comique*, *Comédie Italienne*, *Comédie Française*, *Théâtre Italien* and *Théâtre de Monsieur*.[1]   On the concert side, the *Concert spiruel* (1725–91) had few serious rivals till towards the end of the century, when its position was challenged, first by the *Concert des Amateurs* (1770), and later on by the *Concert de la Loge Olympique*.

Eighteenth century France was not without its private musical establishments. These were very similar to those at the German courts, although not on so large a scale. The Duc d'Orléans, La Pouplinière, the Prince de Conti, the Duc de Noailles and others employed small groups of professional musicians who provided entertainment for their friends and added artistic lustre to the splendid homes of the French aristocracy. The concerts of La Pouplinière (from about 1731 to 1762) were certainly influential in bringing to France a taste for the symphony as it was being developed in Germany round about the middle of the century.

The music in the provincial towns of France seems to have been little more than a pale reflection of the activities of the capital. Most of the larger towns had theatres, and in these, no doubt, small orchestras were employed. Almost every town of any pretension had its concert-society, in the performances of which amateurs and professional musicians joined, but none of them appear to have been able to maintain a permanent orchestra. The music of France was the music of Paris.

The opera orchestra at Paris in the early decades of the 18th century was still organised on the basis which had become stabilised in Lulli's time. The works they played, namely, operas and ballets by Lulli and his immediate successors,[2] were scored in the Lullian style for five-part strings, including *viole da*

---

[1] Known later (1791) as the *Théâtre de la rue Feydeau*.

[2] Colasse, Campra, Desmarets, Destouches, Montéclair, Mouret, etc.

gamba, with parts for flutes, oboes and bassoons, and trumpets and drums for special occasions. The list of 1713 (p. 24) shows the already out-of-date constitution of the orchestra at that time. Although no list is available, the orchestra evidently retained its old-fashioned constitution during the 'twenties. The same operas and ballets were performed, and when Quantz arrived in Paris in 1726 there were still at least two *gamba* players in the orchestra, by name, Fortcroix and Roland Marais.[1] The leading violinists were then Baptiste Anet (d. 1755) and Pierre Guignon (1702–1774).[2] The flautists were Michel Blavet (1700–68), Lucas, the brothers Braun and J. Ch. Naudot, of which the most famous was Blavet. Although there was no lack of good players in it, in Quantz's opinion, the playing of the opera orchestra was then "bad."[3] They played by ear and from memory more than from the music, and were only kept in order by a time-beater armed with a big stick.

Just about this time (1725) the *Concert spirituel* was founded for the purpose of giving concerts when the *Opéra* was closed. They were held in a room (*Salle des Suisses*) in the Tuileries. The first violinist-leader was Anet, who was succeeded in 1738 by Guignon, both of whom were also leaders at the *Opéra*, but no list of the orchestra is available. While the *Concert spirituel* was devoted mainly to French music, at another series of concerts, the *Concert Italien* (started in 1724), only Italian music was performed. These concerts were held in another room in the Tuileries, and the orchestra comprised 18 players, made up of violins, violas, 'cellos and one double-bass, with flutes and bassoons.[4] Quantz heard both the *Concert spirituel* and the *Concert Italien*, and remarked that neither should be despised, but that, of the two, the *Concert spirituel* was the most popular. From the fact that two series of concerts were being held in Paris at the same time, the one devoted to French and the other to Italian music, it may be surmised that French musical taste was then already strongly divided, and that the rabid partisanship which was to break out so violently later on in the famous *Querelle des Bouffons* (1752–54), was gathering force in the earlier decades of the century.

[1] A son of Marin Marais, a great gambist of Lulli's time.
[2] Guignon was the last to bear the title "Roi des Violons."
[3] Autob. Marpurg, I, p. 238.
[4] Brenet, pp. 164, 165, from *Mercure*, April, 1727.

In the third quarter of the century the works of Rameau, Rebel and Francœur, Royer, Mondonville and others of their generation began to replace those of the Lullian composers in the repertoire of the *Opéra*, and the old grouping of the string parts began to give way to the four-part organisation which was already standardised everywhere except in Paris. François Rebel (1701–75) and François Francœur (1698–1787) were both violinist-leaders at the *Opéra* in the 'thirties, and Jean-Féry Rebel, father of François, manipulated the big stick as *Batteur de Mesure*.[1] By the mid-century, both at the *Opéra* and the *Concert spirituel*, the orchestras had more or less shaken off the retarding effects of the Lullian era, and, more open to foreign influence, began to share in the progress which was going on all round them. The string orchestra was re-shaped, clarinets were working their way into the wood-wind group, and the position of the horns and trumpets was being regularised.

A share in the general progress must be placed to the credit of La Pouplinière and his small orchestra, covering the period round about the mid-century.

In 1751 we begin to get full particulars of the personnel of the Paris orchestras from the *Almanach* (see p. 25). In that year, at the *Concert spirituel*, the violinist-leader was the famous player Pierre Gaviniés (1726–1800). Of the other violinists, Canavas, Dupont, Travenol, Piffet and Mangean figure in Marpurg's list of the most distinguished players in Paris in 1755.[2] The flutes and oboes were played by Taillard, Despréaux, Mounot, Sallantin,[3] and Bureau, and the bassoons by Brunel, Garnier and Capelle. Hébert "et son camarade" were the horn players.[4] The only trumpeter named is Stofel, and the timpanist was Vincent.

Of the 38 players at the *Concert spirituel*, 16 were also in the orchestra at the *Opéra*. There the violinist-leader was Jacques Aubert (d. 1753). The flute and oboe players included the famous Blavet, who no doubt was principal flautist, and Despréaux and Bureau, who were also at the *Concert spirituel*; the other two were Sallantin, jun. and Vincent. The three bassoon players at the *Opéra* were the same as at the *Concert spirituel* with the addition of one Bralle. There were no horn players regularly

---

[1] Brenet, p. 193.   [2] *Beyträge*, I, p. 466.

[3] Probably an earlier member of the well-known family of flute and oboe players in Paris towards the end of the century.

[4] Hébert et Saï, probably the same pair, also played at the *Comédie Italienne* in 1751

engaged at the *Opéra* in 1751, and only one trumpeter, named Caraffe, jun. Caraffe, sen. was the timpanist.[1]

Comparing the two orchestras, the most noticeable features are, that although both had 16 violins, there were only two violas at the *Concert spirituel* as against six at the *Opéra*; also that the 12 'cellos at the *Opéra* were divided into a *petit choeur* of four, and a *grand choeur* of eight players, while the *Concert spirituel* had a total of only six. The absence of horns at the *Opéra*, and the single trumpeter in both orchestras is remarkable. The goodly array of bassoons is typical of the period and of French orchestras in general.

The story of La Pouplinière's private orchestra forms quite an important episode in the development of orchestral music in Paris. A large share of the credit for bringing horns and clarinets into French orchestras, and for stimulating a taste for symphony in France, must go to the rich tax-farmer and the little group of influential musicians who made music for him, first at the *rue Petits-Champs* (1731), then at the *rue de Richelieu* (1739), and finally at the *Chateau de Passy* (1747) until his death in 1762.

The first director of La Pouplinière's concerts was Rameau. About 1752–3 Gossec joined the party, and remained in charge until La Pouplinière's death, except for a period (1744–5) during which Johann Stamitz from Mannheim was the leading spirit. When the orchestra was disbanded in 1762, Gossec and several of the players went into the service of the Prince de Conti. It is not till the year of his death (1762) that we get a complete list of La Pouplinière's musicians. In that year the violinists were Gossec (*chef*), Joseph Canavas (d. 1776) who joined in 1741,[2] Nicolas Capron (1740–84), Calès and Miroglio.[3] Carlo Graziani (d. 1787) was the 'cellist, and one Louis, whose identity is very vague, played the double-bass as well as the horn. Schencker doubled on the harp and horn, and yet another harpist was Georges Adam Goepffert. Mme Gossec played the *Clavecin*. The flautist was Le Clerc,[4] and Ignace Cézar (d. 1778) played the oboe. The two clarinet players were Gaspard Procksch[5] and Flieger, and Saint-Suire played the bassoon.

---

[1] According to Marpurg's list of 1755, the two Caraffes played the horns.

[2] Ad. Adam, *Derniers Souvenirs*.

[3] There were two musicians of this name: Pierre and Jean-Baptiste. Six symphonies *A grande orchestre*, Op. X, by "Mr. Miroglio" were published in Paris. Cucuel conjectures that it was Pierre who played in La Pouplinière's orchestra.

[4] Son of an instrument-maker of that name (Marpurg, I, p. 473).

[5] Procksch and Schencker were composers of published symphonies.

In spite of the careful and exhaustive researches of Cucuel[1] it has not been established with certainty when these horn and clarinet players joined La Pouplinière's orchestra, nor whether it was he who brought them to Paris in the first instance. But it is tolerably certain that La Pouplinière had these instruments in his orchestra early in the 'fifties, and it cannot be questioned that by the end of that decade the horns had gained a secure footing in the Paris orchestras, and that the use of clarinets was steadily growing.

The following are some of the horn players of Paris during the 'fifties:[2]

$c.$ 1750. Syryyneck and Steinmetz (Stamitz).

1751. Hébert and Saï (*Comédie Italienne*).

1753. Pétia and Grillet (*Concert spirituel*).

1753. Coltu and Grillet (*Comédie Italienne*).

1754. Hébert and Steinmetz (*Opéra comique*).

1756. Ebert and Grillet (*Concert spirituel*).

1756. Brenner and Schmith (*Comédie Italienne*).

1757. Chindelor and Adam (*Opéra comique*).

It is difficult to find an unprejudiced comment on the playing of the Paris orchestras just after the middle of the century. The *Querelle de Bouffons* was then in full swing, and the partisans of Italian music could see nothing good in anything connected with French music. In 1754, Rousseau, who was strongly anti-French, gave no less than ten reasons why the orchestra of the Paris *Opéra*, although one of the largest in Europe, was one of the least effective.[3] Grimm and other opponents of French music delighted in making fun of the thumping time-beater at the *Opéra*. No doubt there was much exaggeration in these diatribes, and as some of the writers were obviously not fully qualified to give a fair judgment, their views need not be taken very seriously.

Burney, who was no admirer of French music, visited Paris in 1770, and heard performances both at the *Opéra* and at the *Concert spirituel*. He could find nothing to say about the orchestra at either place, but expressed great admiration for the oboe-playing at the Italian theatre.[4]

---

[1] *Études* (1913) and *La Pouplinière* (1913).

[2] Mostly from the *Almanach historique du Théâtre ou Calendrier historique et chronologique de tous les Spectacles.* Some of the names are obviously misspelt. Ebert and Hébert are, no doubt, the same.

[3] *Dictionnaire*, art. *Orchestre*.

[4] André and Krettlay were oboists at the *Comédie Italienne* in 1773 (*Almanach*).

The lists of 1773[1] will represent the Paris orchestras more or less as they were known to Gluck (1774) and Mozart (1778). At the *Concert spirituel* Gaviniés and Leduc were in charge, with Capron as leader. The violins had increased in number to 13 firsts and 11 seconds, with only four violas to balance them. Amongst the violins were Imbault and Venier, who with Leduc were also important music-publishers in Paris. The four viola players included D. P. Pieltain[2] (1754–1833), who later played in the orchestra at the Hanover Square Rooms in London, and at Vauxhall Gardens. At the head of the 'cellos was Jean Louis Duport (1749–1819), brother of the Duport at Berlin, who systematised the fingering and technique of 'cello-playing. J. Felix Rault (1736–*c*. 1800) and Duverger played the flute, and one of the Besozzis[3] was solo oboist, assisted by André and Bérault. Two clarinet players appear in this list, namely, Klyn (Klein?) and Reisser. Four new bassoon players, Richard, Petit, Pierre Cugnier (b. 1740, author of a bassoon tutor) and Felix,[4] replaced the old trio of 1751, and Dargent (jun.) and Mozer played the horns. There was now a pair of trumpeters, by name Renel and Braun, and a timpanist named Herneste (Erneste?).

In 1777 Pierre La Houssaye (1735–1818) became leader, and in the following year directed the first performance of Mozart's Paris symphony (K. 297).[5] Subsequent directors at the *Concert spirituel* were: Jean-Baptiste Rey (1734–1810) in 1782, Henri-Jean Rigel (fils) in 1787, and Isidore Bertheaume (d. 1802) in 1789.

At the *Opéra* in 1773 Louis Joseph Francœur[6] (1738–1804) was *chef*, with Louis Felix Despréaux (d. *c*. 1808) as violinist-leader. The 'cellos were reduced to nine, but six double-basses were now playing. Sallantin and Bureau remained amongst the flutes and oboes, but the three others, Pollion, Pillet and Dubois were new since 1751. Only one clarinet player, by name Erneste,[7] had to

---

[1] *Almanach*, 1774.   [2] Brother of the London horn player (see p. 81).

[3] Probably Jerôme, jun.

[4] According to Brenet, Felix Reiner (or Rheiner) (1732–82). The French often knew the players only by their christian names. Richard may also be a christian name.

[5] Mozart's letter, July 3, 1778.

[6] Nephew of François Francoeur, and author of one of the earliest books on orchestration, published in 1772.

[7] Possibly a christian name, and perhaps the same as the timpanist at the *Concert spirituel*. Gossec mentions two Germans named Ernest and Scharf who played the clarinet in Paris in 1773.

hold his own against eight bassoons, three of whom were also in the orchestra at the *Concert spirituel*. The other five bassoons at the *Opéra* were Bralle, Dard, Lemarchand, Garnier and Parisot. The pair of horn players were Mozer and Sieber,[1] the latter another of the Paris players who combined orchestral playing with music publishing. The two Caraffes remained at their posts as trumpeter and timpanist. Perhaps it was the trumpeting Caraffe who was referred to by Gossec when he wrote (of events in 1773) that: "There was only one large cavalry trumpet available at the *Opéra*, and this was blown by a man who was not a musician."

The above were the regular members of the orchestra at the *Opéra*, but it should not be understood that they were all required at every performance, nor that extra players were not engaged when necessary. A second clarinet and second trumpet and trombones would be required for some of the works produced at the *Opéra* in the 'seventies.

In 1778, Mozart, coming straight from Mannheim where he had heard the disciplined playing of the orchestra there, was not at all pleased with the playing at the *Concert spirituel*. Regarding his symphony which he composed for these concerts, he wrote to his father: "I was very nervous at the rehearsal, for never in my life have I heard a worse performance. You have no idea how they twice scraped and scrambled through it. I was really in a terrible way and would gladly have had it rehearsed again, but as there was so much else to rehearse, there was no time left. So I had to go to bed with an aching heart and in a discontented and angry frame of mind."[2] Whatever its orchestras were like, the French capital was becoming more and more important as a musical centre in the 'seventies. Composers were anxious and ready to produce their works there, and all famous virtuosi visited the city. Another musical war was in progress, this time between the Gluckists and Piccinists. "The concerts in Paris," wrote Schubart, "are amongst the first in the world. The *Concert spirituel* is the centre of all that is big in music."[3] Michael Kelly was in Paris in 1787, and was greatly impressed with the staging and the choruses at the *Opéra*, where "the orchestra was most minutely attended to, and more numerous than even that of

---

[1] Jean Georges Sieber (1734–1815), published early symphonies by Haydn and Mozart.

[2] Letter, July 3, 1778.   [3] Schubart, p. 160.

San Carlo at Naples; but the principal singers (God save them) made a shriek louder than I thought any human beings capable of producing."[1]

In 1790, the last year of the *Concert spirituel*, Joseph Le Gros was in charge, and Bertheaume led the violins.   Joh. Georg Wunderlich (1755–1819)[2] was amongst the flautists, and André[3] and Garnier played the oboe.   Erneste and Chélard[4] were the clarinet pair, and Perret, Richard and Tulou made up a trio of bassoons.   One of the horns was the famous player Jean Lebrun (1759–*c*. 1809), and the two Brauns,[5] the elder and the younger, blew the trumpets.   One Mariotti was a solitary trombone player who was no doubt assisted by the Brauns when three of these instruments were required.   Ambezzard beat the drums.

At the *Opéra* in 1790, Jean-Baptiste Rey and Jean-Baptiste Rochefort (1746–*c*. 1815) were at the head of affairs, with Marie Alexandre Guenin (1744–1819) as leader.   Nearly all of the wood-wind were the same as those of the *Concert spirituel*, but the *Opéra* could draw on two more oboists and two more bassoonists. In the following year (1791) the great player Jean Xavier Lefèvre (1763–1829) was to become the principal clarinet player.   Another well-known horn player, Heinrich Domnich (1767–1844), one of a horn-playing family from Würzburg, played with Lebrun, Buch and Kenn, and between them the brothers Braun and one Jacobé managed both the trumpet and the trombone parts.

Other well-known wind players in Paris at that time were: Hugot (flute), Othon Vandenbrock and Frédéric Duvernoy (horns) at the *Théâtre de la rue Feydeau*, and Ozi (bassoon) at the *Théâtre Italien*.   Several of the players mentioned in these last few pages became professors at the *Conservatoire de Musique* when that institution was founded in 1795.

The *Concert des Amateurs* (1770–81) organised and directed, first by Gossec, and later on by Saint-Georges, played in the *Hôtel de Soubise*.   A large orchestra, which included 40 violins, 12 'cellos, 8 double-basses, with flutes, oboes, clarinets, bassoons, horns and trumpets,[6] gave special attention to instrumental

[1] Reminiscences I, p. 284.

[2] Joint author with Hugot of an important flute tutor (1804).

[3] Mozart (Letter, April 4, 1787) wrote of "young André," a pupil of Fiala, who played "a thousand times better" than the famous oboe player Fischer.

[4] Father of the composer.

[5] Two Germans, mentioned by Gossec (1773), who also played trombones.

[6] Brenet, p. 361.

music, and included in their programmes many of the symphonies and concertos by composers of the Mannheim school. Many of Gossec's later symphonies were written for these concerts.

After the demise of the *Concert des Amateurs*, a very similar society came into existence under the name *Concert de la Loge Olimpique*, and in 1786 settled down in one of the halls in the Tuileries. These concerts are best remembered because it was for them that Haydn composed his so-called "Paris symphonies" in 1784–89.

*   *   *

Like other capitals, London had its court musicians. Of these, the instrumental players formed what was called the King's (or Queen's) Band,[1] a group of 24 players which, at the beginning of the 18th century, was under the direction of a violinist-leader, Mr. John Eccles.[2] His successors were Dr. Maurice Greene in 1745, Dr. William Boyce in 1755, John Stanley in 1779 and William Parsons in 1786.

While the official records supply the names of the players in the King's Band, they do not state what instruments were played. The records of the first half of the century contain the names of several musicians who can be identified as violinists, and three or four who are known to have been wind instrument players; but it is not safe to take for granted that the latter played wind instruments in the King's Band. Amongst the violinists employed between 1710 and 1755 were Henry Eccles, John Banister (jun.) also leader at Drury Lane, John Lenton (flute and violin), William Corbett, also leader at the King's theatre in the Haymarket, William Babell, Michael Festing, also leader at the King's theatre and Ranelagh, Abrahame Browne, also at Ranelagh, and Christian Steffkin. John Shore,[3] who had been associated as a trumpeter with Purcell, and became Sergeant-trumpeter in 1707, was a member of the King's Band early in the century, and his name remained in the lists until his death in 1752. The name of Valentine Snow, who succeeded John Shore

---

[1] The members of the King's Band were "musicians"; the adult singers of the Chapel Royal were "gentlemen," and the boys were "children."

[2] It is not considered necessary to repeat here the dates of the birth and death of the London musicians. As far as they are known, they are to be found in the standard English books, Burney's and Hawkins' Histories, Grove's Dictionary, etc.

[3] Shore was also lutenist in the Chapel Royal.

as Sergeant-trumpeter and is associated with Handel's trumpet parts, appears in the records of 1748. The name of Thomas Vincent, an oboe player, figures in the records from 1735. The King's Band was a uniformed body whose duty it was to play at court balls, birthday odes and other royal occasions.

The main stream of English music, however, did not flow along the channel of its court music. The scenes of musical activity were the theatres, concert-rooms and pleasure gardens of London, with a few outlying centres, such as Dublin, Edinburgh and Bath.

Opera and oratorio found their homes in the London theatres: the King's theatre in the Haymarket (1705), Covent Garden theatre (1732), Lincoln's Inn Fields theatre (1732), Drury Lane theatre, the small theatre in the Haymarket, and others less important all had their orchestras, off and on, large or small, good or bad. Subscription and Benefit concerts innumerable took place at Hickford's room (1713), and at the Concert room in Villars Street; in the city at the Castle, Paternoster Row, and the Swan, Exchange Alley, Cornhill; at the Crown and Anchor tavern in the Strand; at Carlyle House, Soho Square, and other places where suitable rooms were to be hired. The later concert rooms, The Pantheon (1772), Hanover Square Rooms (1775) and Freemason's Hall were the scenes of many concerts in which orchestral music was mixed up with vocal items, notably the Bach-Abel concerts (1764), the Professional concerts (1783) and the famous Haydn-Salomon concerts of 1791 and 1794. These last three were the nearest approach to the modern symphony concert that was reached in London during the 18th century. The principal pleasure gardens at Vauxhall (1732), Ranelagh (1742) and Marylebone (1738) took an important part in London's music-making, and there oratorio, vocal and instrumental items and other entertainments of all sorts were mixed up in a glorious medley of music, serious and trivial. The Prince of Wales' Sunday concerts at Carlton House in the 'eighties and those of the Anacreontic Society at the Crown and Anchor tavern about the same time are typical of how Royalty and Society in London managed to combine their enjoyment of music with that of food and drink. The directors of all these performances, corresponding to the German *Kapellmeister*, included at various times nearly all the composers and instrumentalists, native and alien, who passed through or settled for some time in London; a

vast procession of names remembered and forgotten, drawn to
London by the magnets which no 18th century musician pre-
tended to ignore—fame and money—make up the roll of the so-
called conductors who took charge of London's performing
bodies.   More often than not, the director of a performance was
the composer of the music.

When we search the English musical literature of the 18th
century, the Histories of Burney and Hawkins, the dictionaries
and books written by those who were in a position to tell us
something about the English orchestras of their time, we search
almost in vain.   They tell us enough about the composers and
their works, the solo instrumentalists and their concertos, and
more than enough about the vocalists and their voices, but
hardly throw us a word about the corporate playing of the
instrumentalists.   That an orchestra played well or badly means
very little to us because a common standard of performance is
lacking.   Yet we can find ample and detailed accounts of how
this or that famous and forgotten vocalist executed their "divi-
sions" and "shakes."[1]   In their eyes the orchestra was little more
than an adjunct to vocal music, fit to accompany an aria or a
concerto, fit to play an overture or an act-tune which was barely
listened to, but not worth serious or detailed comment for its
own sake.

Quantz was in London in 1727, and found Italian opera in full
bloom at the King's theatre.   The orchestra, he wrote,[2] consisted of Germans, Italians and a couple of Englishmen, with
Castrucci as leader.   All together, under Handel's direction, they
made "an extremely fine effect."[3]   He then went on to describe
the rivalry between Handel and Buononcini, and between
Faustina and Cuzzoni, but before dismissing the subject remembered to record that Wiedemann and Festin (Jack Festing)
were the flautists.

Even near the close of the century, when the symphonies
played at the Professional and the Haydn-Salomon concerts
must surely have drawn some attention to the rendering they
received, the orchestral playing, as such, is only very briefly
noticed.   Thus, when the King's theatre was being rebuilt after
having been destroyed by fire, and the Italian opera was

---

[1] "It has been jocosely said that a singer cannot come out of a song, any more
than a dog out of water, without a good shake" (Parke's Memoirs).

[2] Autob., Marpurg, I, p. 241.   [3] *"eine überaus gute Wirkung."*

temporarily transferred to the Pantheon, the *Morning Chronicle* of February 19, 1791 informed its readers that "the orchestra of the Pantheon is composed of the Professional Band; but never was the execution of that admirable band so stifled and drowned as in the well into which they have been thrust." After the first Haydn-Salomon concert on March 11th of that year, the same paper granted that the orchestra played "with admirable correctness." But if Haydn was satisfied with the playing of his symphonies, he found the orchestra at Covent Garden "sleepy," and on his second visit to London in 1794–5 he criticised the orchestral playing at the King's theatre thus: "The orchestra is larger this year than before, but just as mechanical and indiscreet in accompanying, and just as badly placed."

If we cannot learn much about the corporate efforts of the London instrumentalists, we can, at any rate, find out more or less who they were, and when and where they played.

Of the succession of violinist-leaders in London, from just before Handel's time up to Haydn's visits near the close of the century, the following seem to have been the most important: William Corbett, leader at the opening of the King's theatre in 1705, also in the King's Band; Carbonelli, at the King's theatre, successor to Banister at Drury Lane in 1735, and associated with Handel; Castrucci, at the King's theatre till 1737, also one of Handel's leaders, and, incidentally, the subject of Hogarth's "Enraged Musician"; Veracini and Pasquali, who appeared at various times as soloists and leaders in London during Handel's time; Michael Festing, at the King's theatre from 1737, also at Ranelagh (1742) and the Swan tavern concerts; John Clegg, another of Handel's leaders after Castrucci; Richard Charke at Drury Lane about 1740; William Defesch at Marylebone, 1748; and Richard Collet at Vauxhall. The principal leaders after the middle of the century were: Abram Brown (no doubt the Abrahame Browne of the King's Band) successor to Festing at Ranelagh (1752), and also at the Swan tavern concerts; Giardini, in the 'fifties and 'sixties at the King's theatre, also at Drury Lane, Marylebone (1769) and Vauxhall; Baumgarten, at Covent Garden; Barthelemon, at the King's theatre, Vauxhall (1783), Marylebone (1770) and the Academy of Antient Music; Pieltain, at Vauxhall; G. Ashley, at Ranelagh; W. Cramer from Mannheim, at the King's theatre and the Pantheon in the 'seventies, also at the Professional Concerts and in the King's Band; Salomon, from the 'eighties, at the Hanover Square Rooms, Pantheon, and the initiator of the Haydn-Salomon concerts in 1791.

Only a few viola players can be identified: William Shield, at the King's theatre and composer of many English operas; Salomon, Kammel and Richard Ashley, all towards the end of the century. The leading 'cello players in the London orchestras were: first, Caporale, at the King's theatre and Ranelagh; Pasqualino, Filippo Mattei ("Pipo"), King's theatre, c. 1721; Cervetto, sen. and jun.; later on, Mara and Crosdil of the King's Band and other concerts from about 1764. Abel, the composer, was amongst the last of the *viola da gamba* players in London. A few double-bass players names crop up: Storace, at the King's theatre; Billington at Drury Lane; Boyce, and the famous Dragonetti.

The leading flute players in London were: Loeillet, at the King's theatre, from 1705; Jack Festing and Weidemann, at the King's theatre under Handel; and Ballicourt. In the second half of the century: Florio (from Dresden), c. 1760 at the King's theatre; Tacet, from c. 1756, both the latter associated with the addition of foot-keys to the flute; Graef or Graff; Andrew Ashe (Salomon concerts); and Monzani, later well known as a London flute-maker.

Of the oboe players in London in the 18th century we hear of: Kytsch,[1] for long at the King's theatre; San Martini, from c. 1726 at the King's theatre; Galliard, one of Handel's oboe players; Richard Vincent, for 30 years at Covent Garden, also at Vauxhall; his son, Thomas Vincent, King's theatre, Covent Garden, Vauxhall, and in the King's Band (both pupils of San Martini); Simpson, at Covent Garden. In the second half of the century: Weichsel, at the King's theatre; the famous player Fischer,[2] Bach-Abel concerts, Vauxhall, and in the King's Band, during the 'seventies and 'eighties; the brothers, John Parke, Drury Lane, Vauxhall and Marylebone, and William T. Parke,[3] Covent Garden and Vauxhall; Patria, in the 'eighties; and Harrington at the Haydn-Salomon concerts.

Traces of clarinet players are naturally not many, but it appears that Carl Barbandt and Carl Weichsel played the clarinet as

---

[1] The poverty of his children after his death brought about the founding of the Royal Society of Musicians.

[2] Severely criticised by Mozart (Letter, April 4, 1787).

[3] Author of the Memoirs.

well as the oboe, and were possibly the first regular clarinet players established in London.[1]   Rather later we hear of Mahon and Hartmann in the 'eighties.

The earlier bassoon players were: Karba, J. F. Lampe, Hebden (also 'cello) at Vauxhall, *c.* 1740–50, and Miller at Ranelagh; these were followed by Baumgarten, Parkinson,[2] Ashley[3] at Covent Garden, Schwartz, Holmes at the King's theatre, Vauxhall and Haydn-Salomon concerts, and John Mackintosh.

Very few of London's horn players can be named, although there must have been a succession of competent players available from fairly early in the century, even if only to play Handel's horn parts.   A "Mr. Winch" is said to have been one of Handel's horn players, and we find traces of a certain "Mr. Charles, the Hungarian," who played several wind instruments in London, Dublin and Edinburgh round about the mid-century.   Later on we hear of the brothers Leander and Pieltain.[4]   It is probable that Seipts and ·Rathyen were the two horn players who played with the clarinets in Marylebone Gardens in the 'sixties.   Horns were also played in the open air in some of the London pleasure gardens, and in boats on the river.

The leading trumpet players in London were, first, John Shore, and in Handel's time, Valentine Snow, both of them Sergeant-trumpeters in their time.   Pohl mentions Adcock and Jones in the 'sixties, and in the 'seventies and 'eighties "Mr. Sarjant" seems to have been the leading trumpeter.   Hyde, the sponsor of the English slide-trumpet, appears in the 'nineties.

For a grand summary of London's orchestral players round about 1784, the reader is referred to Burney's "Account of the Musical Performances in Westminster Abbey and the Pantheon . . . in Commemoration of Handel."   There, indeed, is a feast of names for anyone who has sufficient curiosity and time to spend in searching for more particulars of the lives and activities of some 244 of London's orchestral musicians.[5]

Such were the musicians who in far back days took part in the "first performances" of many of Handel's works, of Haydn's last and best symphonies, and of countless transient works which

[1] Messrs. Frickler, Henniz, Seipts, and Rathyen played on "the Clarinets and French horns" at Marylebone Gardens in 1766 (Newspaper announcement).

[2] See Parke's Memoirs, p. 142.

[3] Player of the famous double-bassoon at the Handel Festival in 1784.

[4] Pieltain appears in the frontispiece of Burney's History, Vol. II, 1935 ed.

[5] Some came from the provinces, and some, no doubt, were amateurs.

now lie undisturbed on the shelves of libraries and museums. Bewigged and girt with swords,[1] we may be sure that they refreshed themselves amply after the opera in the King's theatre "according to the custom of the performers at that establishment" at the "Orange Coffee-house on the opposite side of the street."[2] Do they now come in ghostly procession to the Queen's Hall of a night to hear what their 20th century successors are doing?

*　　*　　*

Particulars of Italian orchestras in the 18th century, and contemporary comments on their playing are difficult to find. This may be due to lack of research or to a lack of contemporary books, and these again are probably caused by a lack of interest in orchestral music and playing in a country which was at that time so much more absorbed in the music produced through the medium of Nature's instrument, the human voice.

In Italy, fairly large orchestras were employed in conjunction with choral voices in the principal theatres, cathedrals and churches. In the *Conservatori*, benevolent and religious institutions which gave musical education to large numbers of young people, both boys and girls, performances of vocal and instrumental works took place regularly under the direction of eminent *maestri* and their assistant teachers. These, with the cathedral and choir schools, formed the training ground for most Italian musicians, and from them they radiated in large numbers all over musical Europe. In the palaces and private houses of the more wealthy music-lovers, concerts or Academies, as they called them, were carried out by smaller groups of singers and players, both amateur and professional.

Joachim Quantz toured round Italy in 1725-6 and left a few comments on the orchestral playing he heard in the various places he visited.[3] The opera orchestra at Naples was only "fairly good"; at an opera in Venice the orchestra, led by a good violinist named Laurenti (d. 1752), was "not bad." He heard the music at the various boys' *Conservatori* in Venice, and liked the playing at the *Pieta* best. The opera orchestra at Milan was better than any other he had heard in Italy, especially the violins, led by Teduchini; but the string basses in Italy were not up to the

---

[1] "The etiquette was, that the band in the orchestra, as well as the company in the boxes and pit, should be fully dressed. Bags and swords were then the order of the day" (Kelly, I, p. 15).

[2] Parke's Memoirs. Kelly, Reminiscences, I, p. 316.

[3] Autob., Marpurg, I, p. 223.

mark, nor the wind instrument playing, always excepting that
excellent oboe player San Martini.[1] The Royal orchestra at
Turin (King of Sardinia) under Fiore (d. 1739) as *Maestro di
Capella*, with Somis (1676–1763) as leader, contained some good
players, but was not up to the standard of Milan. So much for
Quantz. In Rousseau's opinion (1754)[2] the opera orchestra at
Naples was the best in Europe; the only other fit to be compared
with it was Hasse's orchestra at Dresden.

Dittersdorf was in Italy with Gluck in 1763, and while at Venice
heard the playing at some of the *Conservatori*. Of the performance at the *Incurabili* he had nothing good to say: "the violins were
out of tune the whole time . . . their *tempi* too, seemed to me
all wrong; sometimes they wobbled, sometimes they dragged,
sometimes they hurried." At Bologna the newly-built opera
house opened with a performance of a new opera which Gluck
had been commissioned to compose. A special orchestra was
engaged, with Lucchini from Milan as leader, and Spagnoletti
(probably the father of P. Spagnoletti who became a violinist-
leader in London) from Cremona, as principal second violin.
Gluck himself directed the performance from the first harpsichord, and the *Maestro di Capella*, Mazzoni (b. *c.* 1718) was at
the second harpsichord. Altogether the orchestra numbered
about 70 players: "At last we heard Gluck's opera, which was a
great success, though the performance fell far short of the composer's ideal. We had been told all sorts of things about Italian
orchestras, but Gluck was not in the least satisfied with them.
There had been seventeen full rehearsals; and in spite of that, we
missed the *ensemble* and the precision to which we had been
accustomed in Vienna."[3]

Nor was Burney greatly impressed with the orchestral playing
he heard in the Italian theatres in 1770. At the San Carlo opera
at Naples the orchestra was generally noisy and rough, especially
the basses: "the double base being played so coarsely throughout Italy, that it produces a sound no more musical than the
stroke of a hammer."[4] The leader, Fabio, "being accustomed
to lead so great a number of hands, has acquired a style of playing,
which is somewhat rough and inelegant, and consequently more
fit for an orchestra than a chamber." The noise made by the
audience, however, was such "that neither the voices nor the

---

[1] Giuseppe San Martini, later in London. [2] *Dictionnaire*, art. *Orchestre*.
[3] Autob., English trans., p. 124. [4] Present State (Italy), p. 365.

instruments can be heard distinctly." This general noisiness was quite in accord with the method of training carried on in the *Conservatori* at Naples. Burney describes the scene at the *Conservatori* of St. Onofrio thus: "On the first flight of stairs was a trumpeter, screaming upon his instrument till he was ready to burst; on the second was a French horn, bellowing in the same manner. In the common practising room there was a *Dutch concert*, consisting of seven or eight harpsichords, more than as many violins, and several voices, all performing different things, and in different keys. . . . The violoncellos practise in another room; and the flutes, hautbois, and other wind instruments, in a third, except the trumpets and horns, which are obliged to fag, either on the stairs, or on the top of the house."[1]

At Milan the opera orchestra, led by Lucchini, "is very numerous," but "the noise here during the performance was abominable, except when two or three airs or a duet were singing, with which everyone was in raptures."[2] Noisy accompaniments were evidently the rule at the Milan opera, for later Burney wrote: "There is a general complaint in England against loud accompaniments; and, if an evil there, it is doubly such in Italy. In the opera-house little else but the instruments can be heard, unless the baritoni or base voices sing, who are able to contend with them; nothing but noise can be heard through noise; a delicate voice is suffocated; it seems to me as if the orchestra not only played too loud, but that it had too much to do." At an *Academia* in a private house at Milan Burney heard a small orchestra of from 12 to 14 performers: "they executed, reasonably well, several of our Bach's[3] symphonies, different from those printed in England.[4] . . . Upon the whole, this concert was much upon a level with our own private concerts among gentlemen in England, the performers were sometimes in and sometimes out." At the church of Santa Maria Secreta he heard a Mass by Monza:[5] "The whole was in good taste, and spirited; but the organ, hautbois, and some of the fiddles being bad, destroyed the effect of several things that were well designed. As a principal

---

[1] Present State (Italy), pp. 336, 338.

[2] "At the hospitals and in churches, where it is not allowed to applaud in the same manner as at the opera, they cough, hem, and blow their noses, to express admiration" (Burney, *Ibid.*, p. 151).

[3] Joh. Christian Bach, who was organist at Milan Cathedral before he came to England in 1762.

[4] Many were published in London by Randall, Welcker, Longman and Broderip.

[5] Carlo Monza, 1760–92, *Maestro di Capella* at La Scala, Milan.

violin, Signor Lucchini is not of the first-class; there is no want
of hand, but great want of finishing. . . . However, such a
performance as this should not be criticised too severely, for it is
heard for nothing." At another church a Mass by San Martini[1]
was heard: "the band was but indifferent; the first violin was
played by Zuccherini, who is reckoned here a good musician."

The opera houses were all closed when Burney was at Venice,
but he heard performances at all the four girls' *Conservatori*, the
Pieta, the *Mendicante*,[2] the *Ospedaletto*[3] and the *Incurabili*.[4] Of these,
he was most pleased with the instrumentalists of the *Incurabili*
under Galuppi. Of the orchestra at Bologna, Burney thought it
"was weak and ordinary," but at Florence "the band was good."

*   *   *

The status of the players in 18th century orchestras depended
largely on the conditions under which they were employed, that
is to say, on whether they were in the service of a court or not.
In large centres like Paris or London, where musical activity was
not entirely dependent on Royal patronage, also in a few German
towns where there was no court, and in many Italian towns, the
position of the orchestral musician seems to have been very
much as it is at the present time. Each went wherever he could
find suitable employment; he could take engagements for long or
short periods, wherever and whenever it suited him. The most
regular work was found in the opera and theatre orchestras. The
concert-giving societies, which could not provide full-time
employment for the members of their orchestras recruited their
players from amongst those who were also engaged in the theatres,
and the personnel of each orchestra varied more or less from time
to time or from season to season, just as it does now in most large
musical centres.

The members of the court orchestras in Germany and Austria
were very differently situated. They were fully and permanently
engaged, and belonged body and soul to their Royal or noble
employers. They were part of his household, with a status
ranging from that of a court official down to that of a domestic
servant. They were salaried and liveried, often boarded and
lodged, and always at the beck and call of the employer. In his
autobiography, Dittersdorf throws some light on the conditions
under which these musical households worked under a sort of

---

[1] Giovanni Battista San Martini, brother of the oboe player.
[2] Bertoni, *Maestro di Capella*.   [3] Sacchini.   [4] Galuppi.

D

patriarchal rule. In the employ of Joseph Friedrich, Prince of Sachsen-Hildburghausen (c. 1751), his status was that of a page (*kammerknabe*) in livery: "The page and I waited at table on alternate days." At Grosswardein (c. 1764) the musical establishment numbered 34 persons, including "nine servants in livery, a valet, a confectioner, besides seven musicians," and they wore a "tasteful uniform." At Johannisburg, in the employ of the Prince-Bishop of Breslau (c. 1771), the orchestra numbered 17, of whom "eleven received an ordinary salary, but the rest were on the footing of common household servants."[1]

We know that Haydn and the musicians at Esterház were in uniform, and that the members of the King's Band in London were given an allowance for livery in addition to their salaries.[2] There is reason to believe that Karl Theodore's Mannheim musicians were also clad in uniform,[3] as were probably most if not all of the German court orchestras.

It was a form of vanity amongst the German princes to show off their musicians, and when they moved from one residence to another, or paid visits elsewhere, they often took their musical staffs with them. Mozart went to Vienna in the retinue of the Archbishop of Salzburg in 1781, and tells how he was boarded and lodged with others of the staff: "Our party consists of the two valets, that is, the body and soul attendants of His Worship, the *contrôleur*, Herr Zetti, the confectioner, the two cooks, Ceccarelli, Brunetti,[4] and—my insignificant self."[5] Gyrowetz explains[6] that he began to write symphonies and serenades when he was in the employ of Count Fünfkirchen in Chulmetz because there the entire household staff, clergy and domestic servants were engaged only if they were musical. Thus, a cook might get a job because he blew a good bassoon, even though his omelettes were not quite up to the mark, and a clerk whose handwriting might have been better would have quite a good chance of being engaged if he could scrape out a useful part on the double-bass.

The duties of court musicians included not only playing in the private chapel, the concerts and the theatre (if there was one) of their noble master, but they might also be required to play for dancing, during meals (*Tafelmusik*) and in open-air serenades. They were not allowed to play elsewhere or to go away on

---

[1] Autob., Eng. Trans., pp. 11, 35, 144, 208.
[2] Chrysander, p. 515.   [3] Gradenwitz, p. 30.
[4] A castrato and a violinist in the employ of the Archbishop.
[5] Letter, March 17, 1781.   [6] *Selbstbiographie.*

musical tours without permission. This permission was often granted, and sometimes the trip was financed by a generous employer; promising youngsters were sent to Italy to develop their talent and gain experience and style. If they had the necessary gifts, the wives or daughters of court musicians were sometimes engaged as singers, actresses or ballet dancers, and many of the sons followed in their fathers' footsteps and joined the musical households when they became competent. When they grew too old for further musical service the old musicians were often pensioned or were given other easy official posts in the household administration. The duties of a German court *Kapellmeister* were manifold. Not only was he responsible for all musical performances and for the training of those placed under him, but he was also required to compose music for the court, and what he composed became the property of his employer. The terms under which Haydn was engaged to serve Prince Esterhazy[1] embraced supervision of the dress and behaviour of the musical staff. Haydn was to present himself in the antechamber every morning to receive the orders for the day; he was required to see that the orchestra was punctual, and that each player was properly dressed in uniform, with white stockings, clean linen and powdered headdress.

Although the musical autocracies of the 18th century kept their musicians in subjection and in a position of social inferiority, it cannot be denied that their rule, whether it was despotic or benevolent, served a good purpose in producing music, musicians and orchestras in greater quantity than the democratic institutions of the same period. They provided the nursery in which the symphony was reared and in which budding orchestration was fostered. They gave the lead to French and Italian composers in using the wind instruments independently and effectively, and prepared the way for Beethoven, Schubert and Weber.

By the end of the century the day of the court orchestra was practically over. Very few of them survived in the early years of last century, when states, municipalities and democratic societies began to take into their hands the maintenance of opera houses and orchestras, and the public began to take an ever increasing share in the pleasures which had hitherto been the hobbies of their rulers. Court orchestras belonged to the period of wigs and pigtails, and died with them.

[1] *Anstellungsdecret*, May 1, 1761.

CHAPTER IV

DIRECTION

So closely is the word "conducting" associated with 19th century baton-conducting, that it will be as well to avoid using it when describing any of the methods of controlling orchestral playing which were practised previous to the 19th century. Conducting an orchestra, as we understand it now, was unknown in the 18th century. The three common 18th century methods of controlling the performance of instrumental, or of vocal and instrumental music in combination, may be briefly summarised as follows:

(*a*) Opera was commonly rendered under the dual control exercised by a keyboard-director, a *Maestro di Capella* or *Kapellmeister*, aided by a violinist-leader or *Concertmeister*, the former being responsible for the performance as a whole and the vocal performance in particular, while the latter was in charge of the instrumentalists. This was the universal custom in all countries, except in France at the *Opéra* in Paris, where a time-beater was employed to mark the time audibly with a big stick.

(*b*) Symphonies, overtures, concerto and instrumental music generally were sometimes controlled in the same way as opera, but more generally by a violinist-leader, who was then in full charge, the keyboard-player occupying a subordinate position as accompanist.

(*c*) When choral voices were employed, with or without instruments, in churches or other large buildings where the performers were more widely scattered, a time-beater, generally armed with a roll of paper, marked the time visually. This method was adopted more particularly when more than one choir or instrumental group were taking part, and were situated at some distance from each other, as they often were in cathedrals or large churches.

If contemporary evidence in support of these statements is required, it can be produced in abundance. The theoretical works, dictionaries of music, instruction books, autobiographies,

letters and general musical literature of the century, from Mattheson to Koch, whenever the matter is under consideration, all
tell the same story, and make it quite clear that the centre of control was commonly at the keyboard, sometimes at the leading
violinist's desk, and that the visual time-beater functioned only
at the performance of church or choral music on a large scale.
Koch (1802) sums up the practice at the end of the 18th century
thus: "In church music as well as in opera, the *Kapellmeister* must
have the score in front of him, partly in order to supervise the
parts and keep them together, and especially in order to give the
vocalists their cues by means of signs. In church music he
beats time throughout, but in opera he generally plays the
figured bass part (*continuo*) from the score on the *Flügel*.[1] In
either case he must give his attention to both the vocal and the
instrumental parts, so that he is in a position to correct at once
any mistakes that may occur. When a *Concertmeister* or leader of
the instrumental music is also available, the *Kapellmeister* generally deputes to him the supervision of the instrumental playing."[2]
C. P. E. Bach (1753) likewise made it clear that opera and instrumental music were generally controlled from the keyboard, and
that only for choral performances was time-beating necessary.[3]

In Italy as well as in Germany the same methods prevailed.
De Brosses (1739) and Rousseau (1756) have told us about the
Italian methods of directing opera and church music. The
words of the former are: "On bat la mesure à l'èglise dans la
musique latine, mais jamais à l'Opéra, quelque nombreux que
soit l'orchestre."[4] The latter wrote: "En Italie, celui qui a
composé un Opéra en dirige toujours l'exécution, non en battant
la Mesure, mais au Clavecin."[5] And again: "L'Opéra de Paris
est le seul Théâtre de l'Europe ou l'on batte la Mesure sans la
suivre."[6] As early as 1704 Raguenet comparing French and
Italian opera, wrote: "On ne bat point la mesure aux orchestres
d'Italie."[7]

From German sources also there is plenty of evidence of the
prevailing custom. Löhlein, in his Violin School (1781) tells his
readers that it is almost impossible for musicians to play well
together in church music, where they are widely scattered, without

---

[1] Harpsichord, piano, or in general, any keyboard instrument made in the shape
of a wing.

[2] *Lexikon*, art. *Kapellmeister*.   [3] *Versuch*, I, *Einleitung*, par. 9, f.n. II, *Einleitung*.

[4] De Brosses, II, p. 378.   [5] *Dictionnaire*, art. *Maistre de Musique*.

[6] *Ibid.*, art. *Battre la Mesure*.   [7] Raguenet, p. 36, New Edition.

being given the beat, as they can in concerts or chambers where they are all close together.[1] Or, as Junker put it: "The *Kapell-meister* in church music is not a player, but a time-beater."[2]

Misunderstanding easily arises when the word "conducting" in 18th century literature is interpreted in its present-day sense, and is associated with the use of a baton: "The next day, he (Mozart) conducted the second performance and then, in accordance with custom, handed over the baton to another conductor."[3] Of course, Mozart did not actually hand over a baton; he had none to hand over; he merely vacated his seat at the harpsichord or piano, and his place was taken by the regular *Kapellmeister*, who directed the performances for the rest of the run of the opera. Busby (1786) defined a conductor as follows: "A term applied to the person who arranges, orders, and directs the necessary preparations for a concert; and also superintends and conducts the performance."[4] But not with a baton. In Kelly's *Reminiscences* we are often told how the "conductor" sat at the keyboard, but never once is such a thing as a baton mentioned:

Dublin, 1777–78. "Signor St. Giorgio conducted at the piano-forte, and Signor Georgi led the band."

Dublin, 1779. "The Band: At the piano-forte, Michael Arne; Leader, the celebrated Pinto."

Rome, 1779. "It is customary for the composer of an opera to preside at the piano-forte the first three nights of its performance."

Vienna, 1786. "He (Salieri) presided at the harpsichord at the theatre."[5]

What the "conductor" did as he sat at the piano or harpsichord is made quite clear by contemporary writers. He played the chords, he helped the singers by giving them their notes or cues, he played the parts when they failed or hesitated, he kept an eye on the whole performance, or, as Busby said, he superintended it, leaving the instrumental playing in the charge of the violinist-leader; he moved his head, or feet if necessary, to give the time or to enforce the beat, but he did *not* wield a baton or beat time with his hands.

The dual control by the keyboard-director and the violinist-leader, if it raises questions as to a divided allegiance, appears to have worked quite well, or, at any rate, quite well according to

[1] Löhlein, p. 55.
[2] Junker, p. 17.
[3] Annette Kolb, *Mozart*, p. 340.
[4] Dictionary, art. Conductor.
[5] Kelly, I, pp. 15, 19, 64, 196.

18th century standards, until towards the close of the century, when signs begin to appear indicating that the old method was becoming inadequate. But for the greater part of the century it is quite certain that when a combination of vocal and instrumental performers was concerned, as in opera, the keyboard-director was the leading spirit and the violinist-leader was his adjutant. In the case of purely instrumental music, however, the responsibility for the rendering rested mainly on the shoulders of the violinist-leader. It seems, in fact, that the performance of instrumental music was more often than not controlled entirely by the violinist-leader, the keyboard-player then acting as accompanist rather than as leader. Thus, we learn from Mozart himself that when he thought the orchestra in his "Entführung" at Vienna in 1782 was getting a bit sleepy, he decided to resume his place "at the Klavier and conduct it."[1] That was a case of opera. On the other hand, Mozart tells us that when his symphony was to be played at the *Concert spirituel* in Paris in 1778, he made up his mind that, if the rendering did not satisfy him, he would mount the platform and "snatch the fiddle out of the hands of Lahoussaye, the first violin, and conduct myself."[2] That was a case of symphony. There can be no question of where the controlling force was situated in such cases. Through Dittersdorf we learn that Gluck also directed opera from the keyboard, but instrumental music with a violin. So, when his "Il Trionfo di Clelia" was produced at Bologna in 1763, Gluck himself was at the first *klavier* and Mazzoni at the second, while Lucchini led the first violins;[3] but at an instrumental concert in Vienna, *c.* 1752, Gluck, "violin in hand, appeared *à la tête* of the orchestra."[4]

K. H. Graun at Berlin, Hasse at Dresden and Jommelli at Stuttgart directed the opera from the keyboard, assisted by their respective violinist-leaders J. G. Graun, Pisendel and Bini, but the Mannheim symphonies were played under the guidance of the violinist-leaders Stamitz and his successor Cannabich. When Forkel informs us[5] that Haydn "spielt zugleich die erst violine," we are surely right in understanding that he led his symphonies at Esterház with the violin, although, it is true, when he came to London for the Salomon concerts, Haydn was engaged to "preside at the piano" for the performances of his new symphonies.

---

[1] Letter, Oct. 19, 1782.   [2] *Ibid.*, July 3, 1778.
[3] Autob., p. 111.   [4] *Ibid.*, p. 46.   [5] *Almanach*, 1783.

That may have been because such were the terms of his engagement with Salomon, or possibly because Haydn was then an oldish man and did not care to face the greater exertion of directing with the violin. It is also highly probable that some composers directed their instrumental works from the keyboard merely because they were pianists and not violinists. When Pleyel was engaged at the Professional Concerts in London as a rival to Haydn at the Salomon concerts, he also directed from the piano.[1]

It should be understood that almost throughout the 18th century a keyboard-instrument was regarded as indispensable in every orchestra. It formed the core or backbone of the combination, and provided a complete harmonic background for the string and wind parts. Contemporary writers make this very clear. To quote only a few in their own words: Quantz (1752)— "Den Clavicymbal verstehe ich bey allen Musiken, sie seyn kleine oder grosze, mit dabey."[2]   C. P. E. Bach (1756)—"Man kann also ohne Begleitung eines Clavierinstrumentes kein Stück gut aufführen."[3]   The anonymous "Biedermann" also insisted as late as 1779 that there must be an instrument in the orchestra on which could be filled out the gaps in the harmony of the string parts; that instrument, he said, was the harpsichord, piano or organ; in some orchestras they used also a harp or a theorbo. No piece could be properly played without the *General Bass* (*continuo*).[4]   "Biedermann" clinched the matter by adding that anyone who said that a keyboard-instrument was not necessary in an orchestra obviously showed that he knew nothing about it.

There is no mistaking the meaning of these words. Even though the music was quite complete on the strings and wind, a keyboard-instrument was always used. The director at the keyboard played the bass part with his left hand, and over it he superimposed the harmony[5] with his right hand, either from a full score or from a specially reduced score (conductor's part), or, as will be shown later, from only a figured or an unfigured bass part.

---

[1] Pohl, II, p. 180.

[2] *Versuch*, XVII, Part I, par. 16: "It is understood that there must be a harpsichord in all orchestras, small or large."

[3] *Versuch*, II, *Einleitung*, par. 7: "It is impossible to play a piece properly without a keyboard-instrument."

[4] Biedermann, pp. 29–30.

[5] Normally in four-part harmony. C. P. E. Bach, Book II, *Einleitung*, pars. 23, 24, 25.   Quantz, XVII, Part VI, par. 4.   Wolf, II, 16, par. 7.

Rousseau defined the process as follows: "C'est l'exécution d'une Harmonie complette et régulière sur un Instrument propre à la rendre, tel que l'Orgue, le Clavecin, le Théorbe, La Guitarre, etc. On y a pour guide une des Parties de la Musique, qui est ordinairement la Basse."[1] Mattheson, Quantz, C. P. E. Bach, Marpurg, Löhlein and several others treated of the art of playing the figured bass in their various theoretical works of the period. It was obviously an accomplishment expected of every properly equipped player on any keyboard or chordal instrument, and one which was absolutely indispensable to the keyboard-director.

The duty of the keyboard-director did not end with merely playing the bass and harmony. He was expected to give to the soloists their cues, and especially to vocalists, in order to ensure their entering with confidence. He had to keep an ear open for mistakes or missed entries, and might have to rectify or supply these on his own instrument, or, in the same way, he might have to help hesitating or uncertain performers. On the keyboard-director lay the responsibility of setting the *tempo*, and of maintaining it by means of strongly emphasised accents, by repeating the chords on the beats of the bar firmly and distinctly, and by movements of his head, arms or body. It was important, therefore, that all the executants should be able both to see and hear him and the violinist-leader, who acted as a go-between. It was because of this that the old writers attached so much importance to the necessity for placing the *Kapellmeister* in such a position that he could be heard and seen by everyone, and to the necessity for placing the violinist-leader and the leading bass player in close touch with him.

C. P. E. Bach, in his well-known *Klavier* school, gave a good account of how the process was carried out, and Quantz surveyed in full the duties of the violinist-leader (*Anführer*) and the *ripieno* players in his flute tutor. Bach was in favour of keyboard-direction, and was probably thinking of opera and vocal music, while Quantz regarded violin-direction as best, and was probably thinking more of instrumental music than of opera. Both of their books date from just after the middle of the 18th century, and both were conscientious and skilled musicians occupying prominent positions.

Bach[2] maintained that it was the keyboard-instrument which

---

[1] Art. *Accompagnement.*

[2] It should be understood that Carl Philipp Emanuel Bach is referred to.

D*

supplied the harmonic backbone of the orchestra and gave the rhythmical impulse to the music. It must be, and must remain, he said, the "time-mark" (*Augenmerck des Tactes*) of the orchestra; by means of it the regularity or evenness of the time-beat was best preserved. The instrument could be distinctly heard by the musicians encircling it, and even in places where the musicians were more widely scattered, and where there had been amateurs and second-rate players amongst them, Bach had heard the whole *ensemble* kept well in control solely by the sound of the *Flügel*.[1] At the beginning of a movement, in order to establish the right *tempo*, Bach advised marking the beats of the first few bars very distinctly by means of repeated chords till the players got into their stride, and also suggested that it might be advisable to play the melodic part with the violins till the *tempo* was grasped. Similarly, in approaching a cadence or a pause, and when resuming the *tempo* after any such disturbance of its regularity, firmly marked chords on the *Klavier* would help the players to feel the throb of the beat and to follow any variation or irregularity of the *tempo* which the *Kapellmeister* might like to make. In the same way tendencies to drag the pace or to hurry it might be checked. Apart from the use of strongly marked accents on the keyboard-instrument, it is also made clear that in some circumstances, movements of the *Kapellmeister's* head or body would help to regulate the playing and keep the *ensemble* intact.

Altogether, one. may suppose that there would be quite a lot of head-nodding in this method of control, and the frequent references to marking the time with the foot which occur in many 18th century tutors rather suggests that the lower limbs also took an active and audible part in shepherding the orchestral flock past dangerous corners.

In theory, at all events, the idea was that the keyboard-director set the pace, handed it on to the violinist-leader and the leading bass player, and that they in turn distributed it to the rest of the musicians. Both the ear and the eye were employed in picking up the intentions of the keyboard-director and his lieutenant the violinist-leader. The importance of the latter as a link in the chain of communication between the director of a performance and the outlying executants is often emphasised by 18th century writers, and one may be excused for wondering if, in this process of handing on the time-beat from one to another, it did not

[1] Bk. I, *Einleitung*, par. 9, f.n.

sometimes lose something on the way. It can easily be understood that the violinist-leader would take a very large share of the
responsibility of controlling the *ensemble* of a body of performers
which otherwise would have little else to guide them except the
sound of the harpsichord and the sight of the movements of
the head or hands of the keyboard-director. This is how the
function of the violinist-leader is set forth in an English dictionary
of music:[1] "A performer who in a concert takes the principal
violin, receives the time and style of the several movements from
the conductor and communicates them to the rest of the band.
The leader, after the conductor, holds the most important
station in the orchestra. It is to him that the other performers
look for direction in the execution of the music, and it is on his
steadiness, skill, and judgment, and the attention of the band to
his motion, manner and expression, that the concinnity, truth, and
force of effect, do in a great measure depend."

Quantz threw the weight of his opinion in favour of control
by means of a violinist-leader or *Anführer*, as he called him.
While he did not insist that the director of an orchestra must
be a violinist, he thought it better that he should be.[2] No doubt
he was thinking more of instrumental than of vocal performance.
In Chapter XVII of his very comprehensive book,[3] Quantz
devoted sections of considerable length to reviewing the functions
of the *Anführer*, the *ripieno* violinists, the viola, 'cello and bass
players, and the accompanying keyboard-player, and made it
clear that the source of control should be in the hands of the
violinist-director. While he did not ignore the importance of the
keyboard-instrument as a harmonic background for the orchestra,
nor its value as a steadying influence, Quantz allotted to the
violinist-director the duty of originating the rhythmical impulse
which carries the playing of the orchestra on its way, thus
reversing Bach's practice, by changing the source of leadership
from the keyboard to the violin. So, instead of being regulated
by strongly marked chords on the *Klavier*, the players were to be
controlled by the strong accentuation and the rhythmic impulse
of the *Anführer's* violin-playing. Instead of watching the head
and hands of the cembalo-player, they watched the bow-arm
of the violinist-leader, and imbibed from him the time-beat, the
rhythm, the phrasing and the style of the music. It can be

---

[1] Busby, art. Leader.   [2] *Versuch*, XVII, Part I, par. 3.
[3] Quantz's book is far from being only a flute tutor.

understood that it was not always easy to establish the right
tempo at the beginning of a movement, at a change of time or
tempo, during a *rallentando* or after a pause, when this or any other
baton-less method of control was in use. Quantz admits that in
his experience it was not at all an unusual occurrence for a few bars
at the start of a movement to pass before the players got hold of
the beat and were able to play properly together;[1] this, he said,
was especially the case in large orchestras, and when the *tempo*
was quick and the notes short. He recommended that at the
start, the players should memorise a bar or two of the music,
keep their bows close over the strings, and watch attentively the
bowing of the violinist-director.[2] Quantz referred to the
difficulty of maintaining a good *ensemble* when any departure
from the regular *tempo* occurred, and to the necessity of checking
tendencies to drag or hurry the pace, just as Bach did. He
insisted on the importance of using the sight as well as the hearing
to overcome such difficulties.

Especially when the orchestra is large and the players more
widely spread out, must they watch the movements of the
violinist-director: "Because sound takes some time to travel, and
cannot be heard so promptly from a distance as at close quarters,
one must make use of one's eyes to look often at the leader, not
only at the beginning of a piece, but also during the course of it,
and in the event of any little disturbance. He who knows anything about violin-playing will be able to regulate his playing by
watching the bowing of the leader. If all the players cannot see
the leader or cannot hear him, they must regulate their playing
by that of a neighbouring player who is nearer to the leader,
and so preserve the *tempo*."[3] Here, again, we see that process
of handing on the time of the music by stages, and wonder if
under such conditions there was not sometimes a tail of the
orchestra which dragged a bit behind the body.

Leopold Mozart also remarked that, if an orchestra is to play
well together, all the players must see one another, and must look
especially at the leader (*Anführer*) in order to play in the same
tempo and with the same expression.[4] Not only the violinist-
leader's bow-arm, but also his left arm and violin evidently took
part in this process of conveying the time-beat from the leader
to his followers. Reichardt[5] described how Pisendel at Dresden

---

[1] *Versuch*, XVII, Part VII, par. 45.   [2] *Ibid.*, XVII, Part I, par. 5.
[3] *Ibid.*, XVII, Part VII, par. 42.   [4] *Versuch* (Mozart), XII, par. 21.   [5] *Briefe*, p. 40.

used to move the head and neck of his violin up and down or sideways to mark the beats of the bar.

Altogether, it seems as if the 18th century violinist-director controlled his orchestra in much the same way as the leader of a string quartet or other chamber music combination controls his little party of players to-day; but that the difficulty of doing so effectively would increase with the number of players and the distance between them and their leader. Much would also depend on how familiar the players were with their own parts and those of other players, on how well they were rehearsed, and on their individual skill and musicianship. But even under the best of circumstances it is hardly possible to avoid coming to the conclusion that, except in the case of very small and compact orchestras, there must have been a certain time-lag between the initiation of the time-beat at the leader's desk and its reception at the outlying fringes of the orchestra.

The violinist-leader, however, has never died out. Viennese dance orchestras have always been directed in just the same way, and many a small orchestra playing light music without any conductor is now led by a violinist who makes just the same sort of bodily movements and accentuates his playing in just the same manner as did Quantz's *Anführer* two hundred years ago.

Some views expressed by German writers towards the close of the 18th century show that considerable difference of opinion existed as to the respective merits of keyboard and violin-direction. Amongst these, the anonymous "Biedermann" set forth his views in his interesting little booklet *Wahrheiten die Musik betreffend*[1] (1779), wherein he describes the various methods of controlling an orchestra under no less than six headings, adding with no uncertain voice his verdict as to their efficacy or otherwise. The whole presents a complete survey of the subject at that time, and is, despite the exaggeration, so instructive and amusing that it is well worth reproducing. Freely translated, the "Biedermann's" exposition, headed: *Direktion eines Orchesters*, runs as follows:[2]

1. When an orchestra is so arranged that all the players can see and hear one another, when they are all efficient, when the composer has provided adequate marks of expression, when the *tempo* is understood, and when the piece has been properly rehearsed, it needs no further directing; it then directs itself, and goes like a clock which has been wound up. This is the true and

[1] Truths about Music. [2] *Ibid.*, p. 42.

free way of directing an orchestra, of which the listener knows little or nothing.

2.   But when an orchestra is not so well placed, nor so well equipped, the direction becomes audible, visible, and more strained. The cembalist and the bass players, on whose part the harmony rests, have to be kept in constant activity, and, in order that the playing of the orchestra may not fall into disorder, they have to play their parts so forcibly that it is easily heard by all the other players, who then can add their own parts to complete the harmony. This can hardly be done unless the bass players make all sorts of movements with their bodies, and the playing then becomes strained and forced.

3.   In some operas they place the leading violinist on a raised seat, so that he can be seen by all the other players, and give him charge of the performance. That certainly looks adventurous enough, especially when the high-seated *Herr Direktor* makes such convulsive gestures that it seems almost necessary to send for a doctor. The elevated violin screams out above all the other instruments,[1] just as if the opera consists of a single instrument, and as if everything depends on it. The high-seated director turns round; the music flags, and the other instruments groan like frogs in a dark swamp. He stops to use his handherchief; the music again becomes dull. This sort of thing, and the convulsive gestures of the director, constitute an amusing side-show for attentive spectators. But is any orchestra ever controlled in this manner? and can it be? There are many objections to it. In the first place, when it is necessary to seat one player higher than the rest in order that he may be seen, it is a fault in the arrangement of the orchestra. Secondly, the first violin always plays the top part of the harmony, or the melody, with or without ornamental figuration. But, as the melodic part with all its possible ornamentation is just like the decorated roof of a house, while the harmony of a piece embodies its essence and is the equivalent of the complete building, it will easily be understood that the violin alone cannot be the instrument best suited to lead an orchestra, just as it is not possible to move a house by pulling only at the roof. This sort of direction is merely grimacing.

4.   A director should be able to give the *tempo* of a piece just as

---

[1] In the *Musikalischer Almanach* of 1782, C. L. Junker wrote of Cannabich in Munich: "He plays with such warmth, and so powerfully, that he is heard above the whole orchestra." But this was intended to be a compliment, not an adverse criticism.

the composer conceived it; he should be able to help any player who wavers at rehearsal, he should be able to correct mistakes in the parts, and he should have the score in front of him and should know it well. As no one can do this better than the composer, it follows that the composer himself is best fitted to direct the performance.

5. In well-established orchestras the *tempo* is maintained as follows: The composer, who always plays on a keyboard-instrument, and who with the bass players is naturally placed in the centre of the orchestra, gives them the *tempo* as he conceived it when he composed the piece; the basses take it from him and the leading violinist picks it up at the same time, and together they hand it on to the rest of the orchestra, just as they received it from the composer; so the piece goes on its course without any interruption. This is the sure and certain way of directing a performance.

6. But where the principal violinist alone leads the orchestra; where the composer has to give way to him; where the leader is accustomed to hurry over some passages and expects the whole orchestra to hurry with him; where he regulates the *tempo* to suit his own violin-playing instead of to suit the harmony of the music; where he hurries so much that the bass players, on account of their thicker strings, cannot play their passages clearly in their endeavour to keep up with the leader; where, when the orchestra is really playing in time and has forgotten all about the leader, it occurs to him to upset the whole thing again by means of comical grimaces, foot-stamping, and so on; and where the composer is allowed to suffer all sorts of vexations; then the direction becomes not only unsafe, but also ridiculous.

So, one may sum up the direction of an orchestra as follows:

(*a*) The true direction.
(*b*) The strained.
(*c*) The grimace-direction.
(*d*) The safe, and
(*e*) the unsafe and ridiculous

Beating time for good musicians is mere pedantry, as it is in the *Opéra* at Paris, and doesn't help matters one bit, because it often leads only to absurdity; it is, however, necessary for apprentices (students). For that reason the ancient Greeks and Romans employed a time-beater, just as we do now in choir-schools."

The "Biedermann" was a strong upholder of the keyboard-director, and enjoyed making fun of the violinist-director. But through all the exaggeration and ridicule in his remarks a few instructive and interesting truths peep out. It is suggested, for example, that it was considered a sign of inefficiency when musicians required a visible time-beat in order to keep them together; only students and choristers needed any such propping up; experienced musicians should be able to play together and keep time without it. Reading between the lines, we can hardly miss the suggestion that in the dual control by keyboard and violin players there was always present some of the difficulty which was brought about by a divided centre of control; we can easily imagine that there might be a conflict between the two sources of leadership.

Schünemann[1] quotes from an article which appeared in the *Jahrbuch der Tonkunst von Wien und Prag* (1796) to show that this difficulty did actually exist: "How easy it is to get into disorder when two individuals are simultaneously in charge, one at the keyboard and the other with the violin. Some of the musicians follow the *Kapellmeister* while others follow the leader of the violins. One can judge what the result is, when, as is quite possible, each adopts a different *tempo*."

Just at the end of the century the problem appears to have become rather acute, and some of the conflicting views which were expressed at that time rather suggest that the dual control was not working as well as it did in the middle of the century. As it turned out, the "Biedermann" was backing the wrong horse when he upheld the keyboard-director and ridiculed the violinist-director. Even as he wrote, the position of the keyboard-instrument in the orchestra was being seriously undermined, and with it the authority of the keyboard-director was being threatened. It was the violinist-director who in the end was destined to develop into the baton-conductor.

The keyboard-instrument in the orchestra, however, died very leisurely; the lingering process lasted about 50 years, covering roughly the last quarter of the 18th and the first quarter of the 19th century. In the 'seventies and 'eighties composers were beginning to lay out their parts in such a way that the orchestra supplied all its own harmony without requiring any support from a chordal instrument. The figured bass part languished,

[1] *Geschichte*, p. 177.

and eventually disappeared altogether. The last symphonies of Haydn and Mozart require no backing by the piano. So the growing strength of the orchestra and the increasing sonority of orchestration overwhelmed what was originally its prop and stay; by slow degrees the support weakened, became superfluous, and was eventually kicked away, leaving the orchestra to stand on its own legs. Even well into the 19th century composers often sat at the piano and nominally directed the orchestra.

One wonders what exactly did Haydn do when he sat at the piano for the performances of his London symphonies at the Salomon concerts in 1791 and 1794. Did he play the chords? Did he actually control the *ensemble?* or was he there only as a sort of figurehead? Who can tell? All we know is that he "presided" at the piano while Salomon "led" the orchestra.

As the keyboard-director lost ground the violinist-director gained power, and his technique underwent slight change. With his instrument in his hand, and ready to play whenever he thought fit, he began to use the bow as a baton with which to beat time; so came into being a form of direction which was intermediate between that of the violinist-leader of the 18th century and that of the baton-conductor of the 19th century. One might call this type a violinist-conductor, because he did conduct. The period of this form of direction lasted till long after the keyboard-director became obsolete,[1] and covers the initial stages of the rise of the baton-conductor. Schuppanzigh, Beethoven's friend and violinist in Vienna, was a typical violinist-conductor, and probably one of the last and best remembered of this type was the famous Habeneck in Paris.

With their violin-playing and time-beating the violin-conductors of the early 19th century mixed some of the interpretative element which so clearly distinguishes 19th century baton-conducting from 18th century time-beating.

Actual baton-conducting of orchestras made its beginning at Berlin in the 'eighties and 'nineties of the 18th century. Reichardt and his successor Anselm Weber were the pioneers who discarded both the piano and the violin as instruments of leadership, and

---

[1] Italian Opera, Paris, 1820: "I became confirmed but the more strongly in my opinion, that a theatrical orchestra, however excellent it may be, on account of the great distance of the extreme ends, should not be conducted otherwise than by a continual beating of the time, and, that to mark the time constantly by motions of the body, and the violin, like Mr. Grasset does, is of no use" (Spohr, Autob., II, p. 118).

began to use silent implements to mark the time, control the *ensemble*, and influence the rendering of the music by guiding the players in the interpretation thereof. It said that Anselm Weber conducted with a baton made of leather and stuffed with hair.

The situation at the end of the 18th century shows older methods of control slowly giving way to the new. The piano still had a place in opera orchestras because it was required for the accompaniment of *Recitative*, but from being the seat of the controlling force its status was being steadily lowered to that of a music-desk on which the conductor's score was placed. The violinist-conductor assumed control of the actual playing, and it was only a matter of time before he exchanged the violin bow for the baton. The precepts of C. P. E. Bach and Quantz lost much of their force as a new technique of conducting and a new type of musician began to take shape. Time-beating and interpretation joined forces to form the new technique, and the process began which eventually split the old type of composer-director into two separate individuals, one of which was to create and the other to interpret the music. Beethoven's life (1770–1827) almost covers the whole period of transition; Haydn's death (1809) may be used to mark the dotage of the old period, and Wagner's birth (1813) the infancy of the new period in the history of orchestral conducting.

While the direction of musical performance in the 18th century by means of either a keyboard-instrument or a violin, or both together, was concerned with both *ensemble* and interpretation, time-beating, whether audible or not, appears to have been employed more as a means of conveying a steady time-beat to executants whose performance could not be co-ordinated without it. The keyboard-director and the violinist-leader functioned musically and artistically, while a time-beater acted more as a human metronome, a time-mechanism only necessary for the control of large or scattered forces.

The custom of hammering out the time with a big stick, which prevailed at the *Opéra* in Paris, is remarkable, not because audible time-beating was at all uncommon in the 18th century, but rather because this seems to have been the only theatre where it was practised. The first intimation we have of this custom is in the story that Lulli died from the effects of a wound which he inflicted on his foot when hammering out the time in this

manner.[1] Even if the truth of this story may be questioned, it is
impossible to ignore the evidence which crops up repeatedly
during the 18th century to the effect that this custom prevailed
at the Paris *Opéra* until some time after the mid-century.

In the English translation of Raguenet's Paralléle (1704)[2] a
footnote refers to the Paris custom of beating time "on a Table
put there for that purpose, so loud, that he made a greater Noise
than the whole Band"; and in 1726 Quantz[3] drew attention to the
inferiority of the orchestra at the *Opéra*, asserting that it had to
be kept in order by beating the time with a big stick. In Baron
Grimm's *Le petit Prophète* (1753)[4] the time-beater at Paris is
likened to a wood-chopper, and, needless to state, Rousseau
missed no opportunity of condemning this French custom:
"A l'Opéra de Paris il n'est pas question d'un rouleau de Papier,
mais d'un bon gros Bâton de bois bien dur, dont le Maître
frappe avec force pour être entendu de loin."[5]—"Combien les
oreilles ne sont-elles pas choquées à l'Opéra de Paris du bruit
désagréable et continuel que fait, avec son bâton, celui qui bat
la Mesure, et que le petit Prophète compare plaisamment à un
Bucheron qui coupe du bois."[6]—"Le bruit insupportable de son
bâton qui couvre et amortit tout l'effet de la Symphonie."[7]
Hiller,[8] Grétry,[9] Castil-Blaze[10] and others have testified to the
disturbing effect of the audible time-beat at Paris, a custom which
continued at any rate as late as the 'sixties. It is not suggested
that the composers of operas ever beat time in this way; the time-
beater's function at Paris was something quite apart from those
of the *Clavecin* player and the leader of the violins, both of whom
were employed in the Paris orchestra, as everywhere else: "A
l'Opéra de Paris, par exemple, l'emploi de battre la Mesure est
un office particulier; au lieu que la Musique des Opéra et com-
posée par quiconque en a le talent et la volonté."[11]

According to Brenet, the time was beaten at the *Concert
spirituel* in the same way as at the *Opéra* till 1762, when a change
was made. Dauvergne, the official time-beater, directed the first

---

[1] Louis Travenol et Jacques Durey de Noinville, *Histoire*, 1757, p. 42. See also,
Burney, *An Account*, "Introduction," p. 14.

[2] A comparison between the French and Italian Musick and Operas, London,
1709.

[3] Autob., Marpurg, I, p. 238.   [4] *Le Bucheron.*

[5] Rousseau, *Dict.*, art. *Bâton de Mesure.*   [6] *Ibid.*, art. *Battre la Mesure.*

[7] *Ibid.*, Art. *Orchestre.*   [8] *Anweisung*, 1774.   [9] *Mémoires*, 1789.

[10] *De l'Opéra en France*, 1820.   [11] Rousseau, *Dict.*, art. *Maistre de Musique.*

concert in the old way, but at the second concert the violinist-leader, Gaviniés, led the performance with the violin.[1]

Even though an audible time-beat was not considered a desirable accompaniment to music, and although it was often condemned in the theoretical works of the 18th century, there seems to be no doubt that it was frequently employed, even if only as a necessary evil, to steady the singing and playing of executants who were getting out of hand.   Time-beating, indeed, is sometimes defined in contemporary dictionaries as a "motion of the hand or foot,"[2]—"mouvemens de la main ou du pied";[3] and, if the use of the foot could be quiet and unobtrusive, there are plenty of hints which show that it could and did only too easily develop into audible stamping of the feet. Schünemann[4] quotes a number of German 18th century theorists who found it necessary to inveigh against the common habit amongst German choirmasters of stamping their feet or otherwise noisily marking the time in their endeavours to synchronise the singing and playing of their choirs and instrumentalists.   Mattheson, who considered that these noisy time-beaters must be "cleverer with their feet than with their heads,"[5] also Führmann, Scheibe, Mizler, Löhlein, Rolle, Petri and Adlung are amongst those who by the frequency of their complaints make it quite clear that noisy time-beating was nothing exceptional in German churches.   It is more than likely that even under the best of circumstances, and under any method of control, the pulse of the music would occasionally have to be forcibly expressed by other than visual signs or movements.   We may be sure that the violinist-leaders sometimes stamped their feet, and we know that even 19th century violinist-conductors could not always resist the temptation of tapping on some handy object with the tip of their bows when other means of bringing their teams into order were un-availing.   Berlioz made capital fun out of Habeneck's habit of tapping his bow on the top of the prompter's box at the Paris opera.[6]

If a certain amount of audible time-beating crept into every form of direction practiced during the 18th century, regular visual time-beating appears to have been confined to the purpose of

[1] *Brenet*, p. 277.   [2] Busby, *Dict.*, art. Beating Time.
[3] Rousseau, art. *Battre la Mesure*.   [4] *Geschichte*, p. 156.
[5] *Exemplarischen Organisten-Probe*, 1719.
[6] *Les Soirées de l'Orchestre*, English trans., p. 123: "A victim of the tack."

controlling choral voices and instrumentalists in churches, and then only on occasions when the performers were many and spread over a wide space. We have already heard evidence enough to prove that this method of control was common in German churches, and Burney[1] told us that he frequently saw performances in Italian churches directed in the same way. At the Handel Commemoration in London towards the end of the century[2] a time-beater likewise came into operation to direct the choruses, and from Parke we learn that a performance of the New Musical Fund in 1787 was under the direction of "Dr. Hayes and Dr. Miller, who, with a large roll of parchment, beat time most unmercifully."[3]

It should be understood that this form of time-beating was considered necessary only for choral movements, and that the instrumental numbers and arias in oratorio were directed in the usual way by a keyboard-director assisted by a violinist-leader. As Koch said,[4] time-beating was helpful particularly in the fugues or fugal movements which so often occur in oratorios and cantatas.

The time-beater's implement was usually a roll of paper or parchment, with which he made up and down or sideways movements, according to old-established principles, to indicate each beat of the bar. The roll of paper is mentioned by many German writers in the 18th century, also by French, Italian and English theorists. Many an old portrait or engraving of that period shows a composer or choirmaster thus equipped,[5] and on the title-pages of old musical works angels or cherubs are often depicted holding in their hands the roll of music as a symbol of the conductor's authority.[6] Some German time-beaters used a stick or staff, others had nothing in their hand, and, according to Rousseau, the *Bâton de Mesure* might be a stick or a roll of paper. Burney mentions "a roll of paper, or a noisy baton, or truncheon."[7]

If to the "Biedermann's" suggestion that time-beating was

---

[1] Present State (Italy).

[2] Parke tells an amusing anecdote about the time-beaters Dr. Hayes and Dr. Miller, and the violinist-leader W. Cramer, at the Commemoration in 1784. (Memoirs, I, p. 39).

[3] Memoirs, I, p. 98.   [4] Art. *Taktgeben*.

[5] Frontispiece, Walther's *Lexikon*, 1732. Frontispiece, Terry, *Bach's Cantata Texts*, 1926. Frontispiece, Denkmäler D. T. (Bavaria), 3rd year, Vol. I, portrait of F. X. Richter, 1785.

[6] Majer, *Neueröffneter . . . Musik-Saal*, 1741, and many others.

[7] An Account, Introduction, p. 14.

necessary only for students, we add Mattheson's remark that "the less anyone understands about music, the more often will he beat time,"[1] we get some idea of the elementary nature of the time-beater's function in the 18th century. Rousseau's idea was that the more time is beaten, the less it is kept, and Burney evidently held similar views regarding the efficacy of time-beating: "it is certain, that when the measure is broken, the fury of the musical-general, or director, increasing with the disobedience and confusion of his troops, he becomes more violent, and his strokes and gesticulations more ridiculous, in proportion to their disorder."[2]   Nowhere is there any suggestion that this time-beating was anything more than a regular clock-like reiteration of the beat, the purpose of which was only to keep the performance intact under conditions where the usual methods of the keyboard-director and the violinist-leader were inadequate.   The time-beater obviously acted as a sort of drum-major.   He was in no sense an interpretative artist whose influence extended to the artistic or aesthetic side of the performance.

The old-style choral time-beater, as distinct from the new-style baton-conductor, survived well into the 19th century. We recognise him in the third party of a species of triple control under which large choral works were sometimes rendered during the first half of last century.[3]   In this way early performances of Beethoven's Choral Symphony, for example, were directed by a keyboard-director at the piano, a violinist-conductor at the first desk of the violins, and a choral time-beater at a separate desk who began his operations only in the last movement.

Looking back on the foregoing survey of the methods used during the 18th century for controlling orchestral playing, we find that they brought into operation three different forces, which may be summarised as follows: (a) Aural control through the medium of a musical instrument, i.e. the playing of the keyboard-director or violinist-director, or both together. (b) Visual control through the medium of physical movement, i.e. the motions of the head, arms or body of the leading instrumentalists. (c) Audible control through the medium of non-musical sound, i.e. foot-stamping, hammering with some implement, or tapping with a violin bow. Basing our judgment on contemporary

---

[1] *Exemplarische Organisten-Probe.*   [2] An Account, Introduction, p. 14.
[3] Vienna, Tonkünstler-Societät. "Dirigent bei der ersten Violine, Herr Ant. Hoffmann; am Flügel, Herr Umlauf; bei der Batutta, Herr Salieri" (Hanslick, p. 94).

evidence which has been supplied, we conclude that these forces were invoked very much in that order; thus, when (*a*) failed to provide sufficient control, (*b*) was brought into operation; and when both were inadequate, (*c*) was employed as a last resort. The present method of conducting an orchestra with a baton, therefore, would seem to be based on (*b*), for it is visual control by means of silent physical movements, but that the conductor is now released from the necessity of playing an instrument, and has his hands and arms free to devote solely to the guidance of those placed under his control. Nevertheless, historically, the baton-conductor derives from (*a*), for he developed in direct line of succession from the violinist-leader, through the stages of playing his instrument and of conducting with his bow, to the stage when both violin and bow were exchanged for the baton. With a baton in his hand, the conductor then borrowed from the principles of the choral time-beater, and united in one person the older methods of visual control while discarding those that were audible and disturbing.

Questions regarding the efficacy of the old methods of control by keyboard or violin will naturally follow a survey of the subject, and comparisons with present-day methods can hardly be kept out of any discussion which may arise. Answers to such questions as suggest themselves can only be somewhat speculative, and comparisons may easily be unsoundly based, for it is quite impossible to reconstruct entirely the conditions under which orchestras played in the 18th century. In the first place, it should he remembered that orchestras at that time played only 18th century music, whereas now, their repertoires comprise an accumulation of the pick of the music of nearly three centuries. Methods which served well enough for 18th century music would obviously not be efficacious for much 19th and 20th century music, and a fair comparison, therefore, almost breaks down at the start because of the lack of common ground on which to base it. Allowing that any question or comparison must rest on the assumption that only 18th century music is concerned, the number of players in an orchestra and the size of the place where it is playing are probably the most important factors to be considered. A large number of players widely dispersed over a large area, as they must be when there are many, must obviously be difficult or even impossible to control without visual conducting. The evidence we have already produced makes it quite clear that this difficulty was felt in the 18th century; hence the employment of time-beaters in large churches where the number of performers was swollen by the choral singers, and when they were dispersed in separate groups or choirs; hence the thumping of the *Batteur de Mesure* in the large Paris opera house; hence the raised situation of the violinist-leader and the central position of the leading bass-player in the non-conducted orchestras.   That the two leading forces were obliged to accentuate their playing strongly, and so force it into prominence, seems to be a confession that keyboard-control was not quite adequate when the players were many.   The proportionately large number of double-bass players in many 18th century orchestras, which has been noticed in a previous chapter, points to a rather undue prominence of the bass part, which is in itself another admission that keyboard-direction was unequal to the task of controlling many players.   When we add to these the abundant contemporary evidence that there *was* often difficulty in establishing the *tempo* at the beginning of a movement, when the time or *tempo* changed, after *rallentandos* or pauses, and that special means had to be employed to check tendencies to drag or hurry the pace, we have some clear evidence that keyboard and violin control was not altogether satisfactory, and common sense tells us that it would become more and more inadequate in proportion as the number of players was increased.

On the whole, it is difficult to believe that the *ensemble* of even the best of the larger 18th century orchestras was quite impeccable, but at the same time we may temper our judgment a little when we reflect that similar faults can and do occur now even in the playing of good and large baton-conducted orchestras.

On the other hand, when the number of players was small, when they were compactly grouped, and when they were playing in less spacious apartments, there seems no reason to doubt that the keyboard-and-violin system of control would work tolerably well, more especially when all players were equally efficient, and always with the important proviso that they were playing the music of their own time.   After all, hundreds of small orchestras to-day play quite well together under the direction of a pianist or a violinist-leader.   Experience proves that, given good musicianship, a suitable grouping of the players, adequate rehearsal, and music in which the steady tread of the time-beat is easily felt, it is by no means impossible to achieve a perfectly good

ensemble with a small orchestra without a baton-conductor. Light
music, which is generally simple in texture and rhythmical
construction, naturally lends itself well to playing under such
conditions, but good 18th century music has also been rendered in
recent times, with no more leadership than can be given by a
piano-playing or violin-playing director, quite as well as if it had
been controlled by a baton-conductor. It is only a question of
carrying a little further the process of leadership which is exercised whenever chamber music with four or more executants is
played. Quartets, quintets, octets, or any such combinations of
solo players can achieve an *ensemble* equal to that of the best of
large orchestras provided that the players are in every way efficient,
that they are well rehearsed, and that they sit close together.
The more widely the players are dispersed, the less successfully
can their playing be synchronised; but even if the parts of an
octet were doubled, given that all other conditions were favourable, such an orchestra could almost certainly, as the "Biedermann"
said,[1] direct itself, and go like a clock which has been wound up.

The conclusion would seem to be then, that, *other things being
equal*, it is mainly the size and extent of the performing body
which must determine whether or not it is possible adequately to
control the playing of an orchestra without a baton-conductor.
The proviso, "other things being equal," however, is important,
and that is just where a comparison between orchestras and their
playing in the 18th and in the 20th century breaks down. These
"other things" are not, and could not be equal.

[1] See p. 97.

CHAPTER V

SCORE AND PARTS

Orchestral music must exist in two tangible forms before it can be translated into sound. The composer must first write it in score, and then each part in the score must be copied out separately for distribution to the players. When there are more than two players to a part, that part must be re-copied till sufficient parts are provided for all the players.

By approaching 18th century orchestras through the medium of the music they played, we shall be enabled to see them from another point of view, and the new aspect will not only confirm much that has been written in the previous chapters, but will also bring to light some information which otherwise would have remained hidden.

There are several good reasons why orchestras can now use hardly any but fairly modern copies or reprints of 18th century works, the most obvious of which is that the old contemporary scores and parts are not generally obtainable. Only a very small proportion of the entire output of that period is available in modern print, and that consists largely of the works of J. S. Bach, Haydn, Mozart, a limited portion of the works of Handel, and some picked works by a number of other composers whose names are more familiar than their music.[1] This repertoire represents, no doubt, the best orchestral music of the century, and for the purpose of performance it serves very well. Historically, however, it is far from being representative enough. Not only that which has earned lasting approval (always a very small proportion of the total output), but also the ordinary work, and even that of poorer quality, must be taken into consideration if we are to see the music of any particular period in its right historical perspective. So, if we want to learn what we can about

[1] During a period of five months, 162 18th century orchestral works were broadcast by the B.B.C. Of these, 125 were by either Bach, Handel, Haydn or Mozart. The remainder were by 16 other composers. At the Promenade Concerts (1940), 72 18th century works were announced, of which all but one were by the four great composers.

18th century orchestras through the medium of the music they played, the selection which is available in 19th century or modern editions will prove to be quite inadequate, and will present a view which is bound to be one-sided, and which may be misleading. That alone provides one good reason for approaching the matter only through the medium of contemporary scores and parts.

Another, and an equally good reason for taking that course is that the later reprints present a view of the music seen, so to speak, through 19th or 20th century glasses. It is just as if we imagined that we could investigate domestic life in the 18th century by living in a Georgian house fitted up with modern sanitation, electric light, telephone, radio, and so forth. The new reprinted score, although admittedly almost indispensable for performing, is clear and precise where the old score may be vague or ambiguous. The new score and parts are, quite rightly, carefully edited, polished and finished in a way which very clearly distinguishes them from the old manuscripts or prints. The new parts are phrased or bowed, and the marks of expression are co-ordinated, or these may be added in a later taste; the old ones will probably leave such things very much to the imagination, or they may be only tentatively or inconsistently indicated. The new score will always specify quite clearly what instruments are required when the old one sometimes leaves us doubtful and guessing. The new part is well-groomed and well-behaved, and would never dream of demanding a note which is outside of an instrument's compass; but the old part may be more perfunctory, and is quite capable of being naughty enough to ask for a note which could not possibly be played. The new score will lay down what instruments are to be used, while the old one may give us a choice. Even if it is in spirit more than in fact, the old sets of parts will get us much nearer to the real 18th century than the spick-and-span new parts; our investigations, therefore, will be confined to the very same old sheets of music, now yellowed with age, which faced the *Kapellmeister* and his bewigged musicians in these far off days.

Certain historical reprints of old music should, of course, not be confused with modern performing editions. The former[1] are generally accurate and dependable; they are intended for study and, moreover, cannot be used for performance because they are

---

[1] For example, the *Denkmäler Deutscher Tonkunst*.

available only in score. Arrangements of 18th century music which are obviously intended for performance vary very much in how far they depart from the original orchestration; in any case, their purpose is clear, and they should not be cited as historical evidence without consulting the original versions. An arrangement of any 18th century piece in terms of modern orchestration and colour is, of course, quite useless for historical investigation, and is just as misleading as the bathroom in a Georgian house.

The music of operas, oratorios, cantatas, etc., circulated in the 18th century largely by means of MS. scores and parts. Only a very small proportion of the whole output was printed in score, and hardly any in parts. Instrumental music, such as symphonies, overtures, concertos and the like, also circulated in the form of MS. scores and parts, but a very fair proportion of such works was published, not in score, but *only* in parts.

Of the MS. scores and parts of the vocal works, large quantities still survive in many public libraries and museums, also in private collections, widely scattered all over Europe and America. While some of the scores are those originally written by the composers' own hands, a large number of them appear to be contemporary copies made, no doubt, for the purpose of transferring a work from one theatre or place to another, the original score generally remaining in the possession of the church or theatre, or perhaps of the patron for whom it was composed. Thus, MS. copies of the same work are often found in different libraries. These copies often differ very considerably, for not only did composers often alter their works for subsequent performances or to suit the resources of different places, but it seems that each producing body was at liberty freely to adapt and alter a work which was no longer in the composer's hands. Different versions of the same work are, therefore, very common.

In such ways, even if it enjoyed some success, music circulated rather slowly and laboriously.

As almost every musician in the 18th century was also a composer, and as most of them turned out musical works in an unceasing stream, the mass-production gave employment to a vast number of copyists. Each theatre, church or court musical establishment had one or more copyists on its staff. Thus, even the small establishment at Cöthen under J. S. Bach included a copyist;[1] from Marpurg, for example, we learn that one Baltz

[1] Terry, Bach's Orchestra, p. 5.

was the official copyist at Stuttgart in 1757, and from Forkel, that Joseph Kinel combined the duties of copyist and viola player at the court at Pressburg in 1783.   No doubt, some of the players in most orchestras were able also to act as copyists, and we may guess that these were, on the whole, musicians who had not made any pronounced success in other directions.   Apart from the regular copyists in permanent establishments who were, so to speak, "on tap," numbers of independent professional copyists carried on a busy trade in the larger musical centres.   In Italy, where very little music was printed, and in Vienna, where music-printing started only rather late in the century, MS. copies of all sorts of works were freely supplied to any purchaser who could pay for them, apparently on a basis by which all the profit went to the copyist, and none to the composer.   Burney tells us of the situation in Italy in the early 'seventies.   At Milan, he wrote: "all the music here is in manuscript," and at Venice: "there is no such thing as a music-shop throughout Italy, that I was able to discover."   Again, in Vienna he found that "as there are no music-shops in Vienna, the best method of procuring new compositions is to apply to copyists."   He tells us also how he was "plagued with copyists the whole evening . . . For everything is very dear at Vienna, and nothing more so than music, of which none is printed."   In Mozart's letters, too, there are frequent references to the copying of scores and parts, which went on incessantly, and, incidentally, we hear of precautions taken by Mozart and his father to prevent the sale and circulation of unauthorised MS. copies of the young composer's pieces.[1]

Rousseau himself was a professional copyist, and included in his Dictionnaire[2] a long article on the subject of copying music, explaining with some care all the details of the craft.

Of the comparatively small number of full scores (operas, oratorios, etc.), printed during the 18th century, perhaps some three or four hundred in all, most of them appear to have emanated from Paris and London.   In the French capital a number of opera and ballet scores by the successors of Lully were printed.   These include works by Campra, Collasse, Desmarets, Destouches, Mouret and a few others, many of them published by Ballard.   A number of similar scores by later generations of French or

---

[1] "Salzburg copyists are as little to be trusted as the Viennese" (Letter, May 15, 1784).

[2] Art. Copiste.

Belgian composers, such as Rameau, Mondonville, Rousseau, Monsigny, Grétry and Gossec also enjoyed the advantages of print. Some of the alien composers who wrote for the Paris public likewise had their full scores printed in their own time. A number of the operas of Gluck, Piccinni, Sacchini, Salieri and others date from the 'seventies and 'eighties, and near the end of the century the Paris publishers issued full scores of the larger works of Cherubini and his contemporaries in increasing numbers.

Many of Handel's works were published in score during the first half of the century, and reprints of these or newly engraved issues were frequently made after his death. Similar works by Arne and a few other native composers appeared in the same form, and these, together with a sprinkling of operas or sacred works by visiting foreign composers, make up a very respectable output by the London publishers in the 18th century. The English publishers also issued in score selections consisting of the overture and "Favourite Songs" from operas which in their day achieved some success.

Full scores were only rarely printed in Germany, most of them in Leipzig, where the firm of Breitkopf had started music-publishing before 1750. Some isolated works by Holzbauer,[1] C. P. E. Bach and a few others are to be found in score with the imprint of German publishers in other towns, and rather towards the close of the century some of the larger works of such as Gluck, Sarti and Salieri, and finally Haydn,[2] were printed in score in Vienna.

Even though a very fair list of 18th century printed scores of operas, oratorios and cantatas could be compiled, it should be understood that they would make only a small percentage of the total output of a period when hundreds of composers could count even their larger works by the dozen. Some 50 operas and as many oratorios, Masses or cantatas, was by no means an excessive record for the busy music manufacturers of these days.

Even a casual examination of the MS. and printed full scores of the 18th century will soon make it clear that there was no general agreement as to the order in which the parts should appear in a score, or that, if there were any such conventions, they varied locally. In one respect, however, all the scores conform to one

---

[1] *Günther von Schwartzburg*, Mannheim, 1777.   [2] "The Creation," Vienna, 1800.

rule, namely, that the general bass part, figured or unfigured, should occupy the lowest stave of the score, and that the vocal parts should be placed immediately above it. This was undoubtedly the most convenient arrangement for the keyboard-director, who played from the bass part and at the same time had to keep a special eye on the vocal parts. Otherwise, the arrangements of the parts fall roughly into two categories, one of which is found in most German and English scores, and the other in Italian and French scores. According to the former plan, the brass and drum parts, if there were any, were placed at the top of the score; below them lay the oboe (or flute) parts, and then the violin parts, although the order of the oboes and violins was sometimes reversed. The viola part was often placed just below the violin parts, or it might be separated from them by the oboes. Below the strings and wood-wind were the vocal parts, with the general bass at the bottom of the score. The Italian-French grouping placed the two violin parts at the top of the score, sometimes followed by the viola part, or otherwise, by the oboes or flutes. Below the wood-wind were the brass and drum parts (if any), and the vocal and bass parts were in their usual places at the foot of the score. In both schemes the position of the viola part is always a little uncertain, and when bassoon parts were included, they appear to wander about the score with no fixed place of abode, very often disappearing altogether when these instruments played the bass of the music, and turning up again when independent parts were written for them. This lack of any very definite and satisfactory plan seems to have arisen out of a conflict among three opposing desires, one of which was to place the parts to suit the convenience of the keyboard-director, another being a wish to place the parts according to their pitch or register, i.e. the higher parts at the top and the lower ones at the bottom, while a third influence was the attempt to group the component parts of the score according to the type of instrument, namely, wood-wind, brass, voices and strings.

In the end, it was the group-system which prevailed, but with the wood-wind at the top of the score, the brass and percussion in the middle, and the strings and voices at the bottom. The convention which placed the vocal parts between the upper strings and the bass part survived long after the keyboard-director, for whose convenience it originated, had become extinct; yet this illogical arrangement prevailed throughout last century and still persists at the present time. There seems to be no reason why vocal parts should now be placed between the viola and the 'cello parts in a score, except that good old unsatisfactory reason—"it has always been done."

Of the purely instrumental orchestral works of the 18th century, an ample and representative quantity survives in the form of MS. scores and parts; few scores were printed, but large numbers of sets of printed parts of symphonies, overtures and concertos were published.

The printing of parts, unaccompanied by a score, started fairly early in the century, but it was only some time after the mid-century, about 1755-60, that it really gathered force and became almost a torrent, when music publishers in Paris, London, Amsterdam and a few other places, poured out a succession of symphonies[1] in parts, of which hardly one outlived the searching test to which they had been subjected when the last three of Mozart and the last 12 symphonies of Haydn became known. If any of them still flickered in the early years of last century, the appearance of Beethoven's symphonies gave them their *coup de grâce*.

It would be unwise to attempt an estimate of how many of these symphonies and kindred works were printed during the 18th century. There are certainly several hundred of them, probably not far short of a thousand. This indicates that there must have been a considerable demand for such pieces, for we may be quite sure that the publishers kept up the supply of these works for no other reason than that there was a satisfactory sale for them.

The symphonies were generally published in groups of six together under one opus number, and some of the publishers also issued them singly at monthly intervals under the serial title "Periodical Overtures."[2] Quite a couple of pages could be filled with the names of 18th century composers whose published symphonies, overtures or concertos are known, in some cases, by only a single copy; even so the list would probably be incomplete. The publishers of these works will make a smaller list, and even if it is not quite complete the following will give some idea of how

---

[1] Often called overtures in the 18th century.

[2] Bremner, Preston, Napier and Wornum issued serial Periodical Overtures in London on the lines of the *Symphonies Périodiques* of Chevardière and Huberty in Paris. Bremner's series ran to over 50 numbers.

many were engaged in what must have been quite a flourishing trade:

Paris[1]	London	Amsterdam
Bailleux	Betz	Hummel
Bayard	Bland	Markordt
Bérault	Blundell	Schmidt
Bignon	Bremner	Witvogel
Boyer	Johnson	*Vienna*
Bureau d'abonnement	Longman and	Artaria
musicale	Broderip	Hoffmeister
Chevardière	Napier	Torricella
Cousineau	Preston	
Huberty	Randall	*Leipzig*
Huguet	Skillern	Breitkopf
Imbault	Thompson	Schwickert
Le Clerc	Walsh	*Mannheim*
Leduc (succ. to	Welcker	Götz
Chevardière)	Wornum	*Venice*
Pleyel		Allesandro e
Sieber		Scattaglia
Venier		*Offenbach*
		André

One thing, at least, we can learn from this extensive printed library of contemporary orchestral parts, and that is, that in the 18th century, in the ordinary course, a full score was not used when a purely orchestral work was performed. It is absolutely certain that, in the case of these printed works, no score was used, because no score was obtainable. Many of the MS. copies of parts were evidently made for use without a score, for there are large numbers of these old sets, now stored away in libraries, which are unaccompanied by full scores. Unless it is securely hidden away or lost, not a single full score of a symphony was printed in the 18th century. The first printed full scores of symphonies appear to have been a selection of Haydn's symphonies published in Paris by Leduc in 1801. These were followed by a similar selection of the same composer's symphonies published by Breitkopf and Härtel about 1806, and some time

[1] It is sometimes difficult to distinguish between a publisher and an engraver in Paris. The French engravers were often women: Mme. Bérault, Mme. Leclair, Mlle. Fleury.

after that, a few of Mozart's symphonies in score came from the same firm. The practice of issuing only the parts of orchestral works in print without the score still prevailed for some time during the early 19th century; the first six of Beethoven's symphonies appeared in parts fairly soon after they were first performed, while the full scores were not engraved till nearly 20 years later, starting about 1821.[1]   In these early editions of the full scores the brass and drum parts were placed at the top, the wood-wind in the middle, and the string parts at the bottom of the score.

In addition to all the old 18th century music which survives in MS. or print, there must have been an enormous quantity which for various reasons has been destroyed.   The critical period in the life of any musical work is that which comes some time after the death of the composer, when his works may have lost any freshness that they ever had, when his style is rather out of date, and when his generation and its taste have passed away.   Newer things occupy the attention of a younger generation, and "poor old So-and-So" is neglected and forgotten.   His works, especially the bulky orchestral parts, are not likely to be wanted again, so they are stored away.   Their value soon descends to waste-paper level; they become mere lumber, and are eventually regarded as a nuisance.   They must be got rid of somehow; so they are destroyed, generally by fire.   It would be useless to attempt to estimate how much 18th century music perished in this way during the 19th century, before it became old enough to acquire historical interest or antiquarian value.   Many old scores and parts have perished, too, in the periodical fires which punctuate the history of most 18th century theatres.   So, by design or by accident, music which is not wanted has been got rid of, and so, presumably, it will continue to be destroyed.

The 18th century printed orchestral parts were commonly a set of eight, namely, two violin, a viola, a bass part which was generally figured,[2] and two parts each for oboes (or flutes) and horns.   Bassoon, trumpet and drum parts occur more rarely till near the end of the century, when they become fairly common. The usual custom was to enclose the set of parts in a loose outer cover, the front of which formed the title-page and included, of course, the name of the composer.   The composer's name did

---

[1] By Simrock of Bonn and Breitkopf and Härtel of Leipzig.   An English edition of the first three is said to date from a few years before the first German edition.

[2] Usually provided in duplicate in the old sets.

not usually appear on the top right-hand corner of the first page of each part, as it does now on all music. The same is found in the case of MS. parts. The absence of the composer's name on the part, if it does not entirely account for the uncertainty which often surrounds the authorship of many old musical works, at any rate helps to explain how such difficulties and disputes arise. It was only necessary for the outer cover with the title to become torn or detached from the parts, and to be eventually thrown away, for the parts of a work to be without a composer's name. In the course of time someone puts a name to them, maybe with some reason, or perhaps merely as a guess. In the meantime another copy exists under the real composer's name, and then the problem is set. We have one work extant under two composers' names; which is the right one?

Under these circumstances a number of symphonies were found under the name of Joseph Haydn which were found also to exist in print under other composers' names, and, as it was considered likely that the printed evidence supplied the correct name, some 40 symphonies alleged to be by Joseph Haydn were rejected by the editor when the complete edition of his works was published by Breitkopf and Härtel.

Another cause of disputed authorship may be owing to two composers having the same name. The title-pages of old sets of parts often omit to give the composer's initials, allotting to him only a title, such as *Signor* or *Monsieur*, and we may be left wondering whether a work was composed by, say, Joseph or Michael Haydn, or by Johann or Carl Stamitz.

Even the fact that a work exists in the autograph of a particular composer in itself provides no guarantee that he composed it. Eighteenth century musicians often made MS. copies of works which were not their own; it might be because there was no other way of getting a copy of a piece which they admired or wished to perform; or, in the case of a young composer, it might be done as a study or exercise. It is not at all surprising that under such circumstances there may be uncertainty as to the authorship of a work of which copies are extant in the handwriting of two different composers, or possibly in the handwriting of one and in print under another name.

Because so many contemporary copies of 18th century orchestral works have been found only in the form of separate parts, they sometimes present problems such as have been suggested, and

which arise so often through the lack of the composer's name
on each part. The 19th century reprint, on the other hand, is
always very sure of itself and gives the composer's name quite
clearly on each part; it may not be the right one, but that does not
prevent us from easily recognising "the hand of the master"
in a work which he never wrote.

A score written at the beginning of the 18th century is
a very different thing from one written near the end of that
century. In the older score a few staves serve well enough
for a rudimentary orchestration in which there is much doubling
of parts. In the later score each instrument has its own function,
and must therefore have a stave to itself. So the score grows
perpendicularly as the century advances. The early score is
liable to be vague, and we may be uncertain of the instruments
included in it, and of when they begin and when they stop playing.
The late score is specific; there is rarely any doubt as to what is
intended. In the old score the violins and the oboes will go
hand in hand for long stretches; one stave serves well enough for
both, and if the oboes are to play alone for a little, it is only
necessary to write *senza violini* or *oboi soli* in the part. The bass
instruments share one stave; the harpsichord bass, the 'cellos,
the double-basses and the bassoons run along in unison till one
of them may be required to drop out or to play without the others;
a word or two will indicate what is desired; it may be *violoncelli
soli*, *fagotti soli*, *senza fagotti*, *senza violoni*, or some such direction.
When trumpets are to play, they must have a stave to themselves,
for they have gaps in their scale, and it is useless to ask them to
play *col violini*. For the same reason, when horns join in, they
must have separate staves. In the late 18th century score each
part must be written on a separate stave, for each instrument has
its own part to play, a part which is not shared with others and
may embody its own technical characteristics. So the staves
mount up to ten, twelve or more, instead of the four, five or six
which sufficed for the early score.

The 18th century composers, whose daily job was composing,
wasted no time over their scores. Every possible labour-saving
and space-saving device was made use of. The framework of
three or four parts *had* to be written, but no one troubled to write
a part twice when a *col violini* or *col bassi* would save labour. It
was the copyist who wrote out each part in full. Even the
printed scores of the 18th century are full of labour-saving signs

or blank staves when an instrument is to play *col* some other instrument. The busy composer who wrote at the rate of, perhaps, two operas, a few Masses and sundry batches of concertos or sonatas every year, could not spend much time over his scores, and he got over the ground quickly in his arias by writing only a vocal part and its bass, with perhaps a violin or a solo *obbligato* part. These didn't take long to put down on paper, and if time pressed, he could always raid one of his older works, or somebody else's, in order to make up full weight in the least possible time.

In many an earlier 18th century score there is no specification at the beginning to tell us what instruments it is written for. The three or four staves look like string parts, and so they probably are, but it is not until we come across some such directions as *senza oboi* or *senza fagotti* that we discover that these instruments were supposed to be playing up till then. In the 19th century editions it is not always realised that in the ordinary course the oboes or flutes and the bassoons played in the overtures, in instrumental movements, in dances and choruses even though these instruments are never mentioned in the rudimentary scores. The contemporary score of an overture by Arne, for example, starts with four string parts and parts for oboes and bassoon, written on six or seven staves. By the time the last movement is reached, the score has dwindled to three staves. Are we to suppose that Arne meant the final movement of his overture, a lively gigue, to be played by only the two violins and the basses? Certainly not. The full orchestra was to play just as in the first movement; the oboes in unison with the violins, the violas and bassoons with the bass, while the harpsichord supplied the full harmony. The copyist would write out all these parts from the three staves given him, and could easily make any adjustments that were necessary if the violin part went too low for the oboes, or the bass part too low for the violas. Sometimes the composer or the copyist did make these little adjustments, but often enough it was left to the players to do the best they could with a part which ran below the limit of their downward compass. Although he gave no authority for his statement, Rockstro was undoubtedly right when he wrote: "In Handel's time, it was always understood, that, in the *tutti* passages the violins were to be reinforced by hautboys, and the violoncellos by bassoons, in much stronger proportion than that to which we are now accustomed, whether the names of those instruments were mentioned in the score or not."[1]

There is much of this rough and ready orchestration in the early and mid-18th century scores. So much of it was just hackwork, and the composer didn't actually write down more than was absolutely necessary. One suspects that he sometimes left more to the copyist than the later composers did. Those who know the music of the 18th century only by the works of J. S. Bach, Handel's "Messiah" and a few oft-repeated works by Haydn and Mozart, see only a limited portion of the picture, a fastidiously selected portion, but not the picture as a whole.

The part in 18th century orchestral music which is most liable to be misunderstood is the bass part. The 19th century editions are apt to treat this as a part written specifically for 'cellos and double-basses; as a purely string part. Up to the time, quite late in the century, when composers did write specifically for these two instruments, only one bass part was written. It was the bass of the music in general, and was not designed for any particular instrument, nor did it embody the technical characteristics of the bowed string-instrument family. In the old scores and parts the bass part is comprehensively labelled *basso, bassi, bassi tutti,* or some such general term; very often it is not labelled at all. The part was intended for all instruments of the bass register, and for all those whose function included playing the bass of the music. The part was therefore meant for the harpsichord or whatever keyboard-instrument was being used; for the lutes, theorbos or harps when they were used; for the 'cellos, double-basses and sometimes for the violas; also for the bassoons. A strong bass part was the foundation and backbone of 18th century orchestral music; weak inner parts were tolerated, but the bass and the uppermost part must be strong.

The old bass parts, of course, all lie within the technical range and compass of the violoncello, for they rarely descend below 8 ft. C, and there is nothing in them which could not be played on the 'cello. The parts could also be played on any keyboard-instrument, but they were not necessarily playable on the double-basses or on the bassoons of the 18th century. Quantz makes it quite clear that the double-bass players in his time were not expected to play every note of a florid bass part, and we may surmise that the bassoon players were similarly excused if they

[1] Rockstro, p. 259.

could not scamper about a rapid bass part on their rudimentary
four or six-keyed bassoons.[1]

Quantz's essay on the duties of a double-bass player in the
middle of the 18th century is enlightening.[2]   In the first place, he
suggests that the players on this instrument are generally musicians
who are not endowed with talent enough to play any other
instrument adequately, and then adds that very few play it clearly.
Quantz recommended using a medium-sized bass with four
strings rather than the old German instrument with five or six
strings.   He advised having frets on the finger-board, and gave
quite good reasons for this; and to the objection that the frets
interfered with the fingering of the semitone stages, he replied
that in any case there was not much difference between the pitch
of a note and its flat or its sharp when the sounds were so low!
When rapid passages occurred, Quantz allowed his double-bass
player to simplify them by playing only every alternate note, or
one of three, or two in every four; the player might make a
selection from the notes of a figure and was shown how to do it
in the examples given:

The double-bass player was specially enjoined to play in time,
not to hurry or drag behind, not to make a scratchy noise with his
bow, and not to miss out a few notes after a rest before he joined
in again, as some players did!   Evidently the 18th century bass
players were not quite up to scratch; or perhaps they scratched
too much.

According to Leopold Mozart (1756) the double-bass generally
had four strings, but the larger ones had five.[3]   About 30 years

[1] Some of the florid bass parts are difficult enough now when played on a fully
equipped modern instrument.

[2] *Versuch*, XVII, Part V, *Von dem Contraviolonisten insbesondere.*

[3] *Versuch*, *Einleitung*, par. 2.

later Schubart wrote of the double-bass that it used to have four or five strings, but that now (*c.* 1784–5) the three-stringed instrument was commonly used for orchestral playing; for solo playing, however, the four or five-stringed instrument was indispensable. Schubart remarked that the large double-bass was very difficult to play; it required the hand of a giant, and that hand should be armed with buckskin (*Hirschleder*).[1] It is not quite clear whether he meant that the player wore a sort of glove or whether his skin became as tough as leather.

The old bass parts are also liable to be misunderstood in that it is not generally realised that they often included the bassoon part, even though that instrument was not mentioned by name. The figures provided in Chapter II show that practically every orchestra in the 18th century, even the small ones, had its bassoon players. From these figures we learn that the instrument was strongly represented in proportion to the rest of the orchestra, considerably more so than it is at the present time. We have Quantz's testimony that an orchestra of only nine string players should have one bassoon, and that another should be added when the players number as many as 20. He reckoned that the right proportion was two bassoons to eight violins. When we read about them in contemporary books, the 18th century orchestras are always well supplied with bassoons. The contemporary scores and parts, however, show bassoon parts written only when these instruments are required to play the bass part alone, or when they play independently of the other bass instruments. The impression is given that the bassoons were used only exceptionally. Dozens of scores may be examined without finding any bassoon parts. In operas or oratorios they may be found in only two or three numbers out of 30 or 40. Hundreds of the printed parts of the 18th century symphonies include no specific bassoon parts. Dozens of Haydn's symphonies in the Breitkopf and Härtel Complete Edition are without them, and of Mozart's 41 symphonies in the same edition, 28 are without bassoon parts, and when they do occur it is almost entirely in the later works written from 1778 and onwards.

Are we to suppose that these bassoon players, who were available in every orchestra, sat and did nothing when all these works were played? Did the Archbishop of Salzburg's bassoon

[1] Schubart, p. 187.

players go out for a drink when a Mozart symphony was played? and did Prince Esterhazy's pair read the evening paper when most of Haydn's early symphonies were played? Did Handel engage two bassoon players to play in only two numbers in "Esther," and were they allowed to be idle during the overture and in the big full choruses? Of course not. They played with the rest of the bass instruments as a matter of course, and only left the track of the bass part when some special melodic or harmonic part in the tenor register was written for them. To the 18th century composer the bassoon was essentially a bass voice. Occasionally he might treat it melodically as a solo voice; now and then he would give it some harmonic part in the tenor register; but its natural domain was the bass. As there can be only one bass part to the music, why should he trouble to write out that part all over again for the bassoons? Of course he never did; it was taken for granted that this bass instrument would play the bass part unless specially directed to do otherwise. And that is why specific bassoon parts are comparatively few in the 18th century scores till towards the end of the century, when each wood-wind voice was becoming more and more independent of the string parts. *Then* the parts for each of them had to be written out separately in the score, and from that time onwards practically every score had its bassoon parts. For the same reason that the composer did not write out his bass part for the bassoons in the score, the publishers did not provide separate parts for these instruments when the symphonies were printed. They did not go to the expense of engraving the same part all over again for harpsichord, 'cello, double-bass and bassoon, when one would do equally well. When the bassoons were to stop playing, or when they were to play alone, it was only necessary to add some direction showing just where they were to stop or where the other bass instruments were to break off. The following, taken from the printed works of Arne, show how it was often done: "Bass, without Bassoons"—"Bassoni soli"— "All the Basses, except the Bassoons." Similar directions are often found in the old bass parts, such as: *Senza Fagotti, col Fagotti* or *Fagotti soli*. It is a mistake to suppose that when there are no such directions the part was not intended to be played by bassoons as well as by the other bass instruments.

The absence of specific bassoon parts in 18th century music has misled most of the editors who have been responsible for

E*

19th century reprints of 18th century music. Unquestionably, all the Haydn and Mozart symphonies, ostensibly written for oboes, horns and strings, if they are to be played as they were played in their own time, and as their composers intended them to be played, should have bassoon parts. It was a poor 18th century orchestra that had no bassoons. The instrument was always there, and it was there not only to play the little solos or other parts occasionally written for it, but to follow the bass part whenever the orchestration was full and all other instruments were playing.

It was only quite late in the 18th century that the flute began to occupy a position in the orchestra on an equal footing with the oboe. Up till then it was more often than not a question of one or the other, but they were not normally employed at the same time or in the same movement. Few of the old scores are without oboe parts, but there are very many in which there is no flute part. It is true that in some of the scores written for a few of the larger orchestras, which were furnished with both flute and oboe players, one may find both instruments employed simultaneously; but, as a general rule, it is a case of one or the other. As Quantz remarked, the flute was regarded more as a solo than as an orchestral instrument: "A flautist has not the same opportunities for playing at sight that other instrumentalists have, because the flute, as is well known, is used more as a solo instrument, and for concerted work, rather than for *ripieno* parts."[1]

In the old oboe parts it is not at all uncommon to find only a particular movement or portion of the piece written for the flute (*traversa*); this, taken together with the fact that many players were proficient on both instruments,[2] suggests that in such cases the players laid down their oboes and picked up their flutes. Leopold Mozart wrote of the opera orchestra at Milan in 1770, that there were "two flutes (who, if there are no flutes always play as four oboes)."[3] The lists given in Chapter II, where flute and oboe players are sometimes grouped under the same heading, support the suggestion that such an exchange of instruments was by no means uncommon. In fact, a certain freedom of choice between oboe and flute runs through much 18th century orchestral

---

[1] *Versuch*, X, par. 14.

[2] The Hotteterres, the Philidors, Kytch, Loeillet, Festing, Quantz, Parke, and many others played both instruments. Kytch played a solo and concerto "on the German flute and hautbois" in 1720 (Burney, *History*, II, p. 994).

[3] Letter, Dec. 15, 1770.

writing, and is in contrast with the 19th century score which is generally rigid in demanding that a part be played by one instrument and by no other. The title-pages of the old printed parts of symphonies and overtures frequently give a choice of instruments. Thus, we find in the English prints that the parts are for "Hautboys or Flutes," and many of the French parts are equally accommodating in allowing them to be played by either "*deux Hautbois ou Flûtes*." The same freedom was sometimes extended to chamber music, and it may be found even in solo parts.[1]

It may be argued that the choice between oboes and flutes, which occurs so often in the printed parts, was a device favoured by the publishers rather than by the composers. No doubt that was so; yet it is hardly possible to believe that it was done in every case against the will of the composer, or that he would so often have fallen in with it if it had seriously outraged his artistic feelings.

The difference in the register of the two instruments is not so marked in the 18th century parts as it became in the following century. Although the natural register of the flute was always higher than that of the oboe, the general range for both instruments in the 18th century parts is roughly between d' and d'''. Solo parts for the flute frequently rose higher, where the oboe could hardly follow; but for ordinary orchestral parts, the two instruments were treated as if they had more or less the same upward range.

That composers were not always careful to keep their parts within the downward compass of the flute and oboe is quite in keeping with the rather casual ways of the 18th century orchestrator. Such carelessness is not likely to occur in solo parts, but it is not at all uncommon when flutes or oboes play in unison with the violins. When the latter descends below d' in the case of the flute, and below c' in the case of the oboe, these two instruments can no longer follow the violin part. Such trifles, however, did not appear to cause the composers any great concern. Sometimes they made the necessary adjustment, but very often they ignored the difficulty, and left it either to the copyist or to the player to deal with as best he could. These little accidents occur especially when the flutes or oboes are required to play *col violini*, and instances can be found in the

---

[1] Some quintets by Boccherini were published for flute or oboe. A concerto by Eichner is for "Hoboe o Flauto principale."

works of J. S. Bach, Handel, Gluck and Mozart, as well as in those of many lesser composers.

The appearance of clarinet parts in 18th century scores opened up an interesting chapter in the history of the orchestra. Few authenticated parts for the clarinet can be found in scores written during the first half of the century. After its appearance at the beginning of the century, the new instrument took nearly 50 years in getting well enough known to assert its claim to be considered fit for admission to the orchestral family. It is round about the middle of the century that we may look for the first signs indicating that such a claim was being made and considered. It was then that the first traces of the new instrument were to be found in the musical records of Paris and London. During the 'fifties the first steps were taken by which the clarinet made a first assault on the firmly established position of the oboe in the orchestra.

It is rather difficult now to understand why the advent of the clarinet should ever have been regarded as a challenge to the supremacy of the oboe. Yet it undoubtedly was so. When the clarinets first began to occupy a place in the score, it was not so much side by side with the oboes as in place of them.

That only one pair of wood-wind instruments should play in the soprano register seems to have been a firmly established idea in the earlier part of the century. We have seen that, as a general rule, when flutes appeared in a score the oboes temporarily retired. Just in the same way, when clarinets appeared, they stepped into the places vacated for the time being by the oboes. The new instrument, it seems, was actually regarded as a variety of oboe. Burney tells us how on one occasion the clarinet "served as a hautboy";[1] in a French *Encyclopédie*[2] we read of a "clarinette, sorte de hautbois," and in Schubart's *Aesthetik* it is described as an alto-oboe.[3] Some, if not all of the earlier clarinet players, were oboists; indeed, the unfamiliar instrument could hardly have recruited its players from any other source. Specialisation on one or other of the two instruments would naturally follow in the course of time, but it was not till the clarinet had gained a fairly firm footing in the orchestra that we hear of the virtuoso players who began to flourish towards the close of the century.

[1] Present State (Germany), I, p. 26.
[2] Diderot and Alembert, 1767.   [3] Schubart, p. 207.

Only rather slowly do the clarinets gain ground in the scores of the second half of the 18th century. The printed parts of the Paris, Amsterdam and London symphonies and overtures admit them rather gingerly at first, and generally with an alternative instrument in case clarinets were not available. Thus, we read on the title-pages and in the announcements: "hautbois ou clarinettes"—"Faute de hautbois, les clarinettes ou flûtes pourront suppléer"—"Deux hautbois et flûtes ou clarinettes"—and similar legends, all of which show not only the gradual infiltration of the newcomers, but also the safeguards which provided against the possibility of their not being available. In the symphonies of Stamitz, Beck, Holzbauer, Fränzl and Toeschi of the Mannheim group, and in the French symphonies of Gossec, the clarinets appear during the 'sixties and 'seventies; in opera scores by d'Herbain (1756), Arne (1762), J. C. Bach (1763), Gluck (1774), Piccinni and a few others, they make tentative efforts to usurp the place of the oboes in a few numbers of the scores.

Already in 1753 Gaspard Procksch and Flieger were playing the clarinet in Paris,[1] and soon after, the oboists Weichsel and Barbandt were helping to make the sound of the new instrument more and more familiar to London audiences.[2] It was certainly no stranger in London in 1764 when the boy Mozart made a copy of the score of Abel's symphony Op. VII, No. 6, in which clarinets replace the more usual oboes.[3]

During the 'eighties it was beginning to be realised that there was a use for clarinets independently of the oboes; that they could be employed with good effect side by side and in contrast with the double-reed instruments. Many orchestras, however, were still without clarinet players, and neither the composers nor the publishers could afford to hamper the use and the sale of their pieces by demanding both clarinets and oboes at the same time. Compromises were still made; the parts could be played by either instrument, or by both simultaneously.

Only when a composer was sure of finding both clarinets and oboes in an orchestra did he write parts for both in the same piece. In some of the French scores of the 'seventies, for example, the two instruments are used together because players on both were to be found at the *Concert spirituel* and at the *Opéra*. Mozart's

---

[1] *Archives de l'Opéra.* See Cucuel, *Études,* p. 17.   [2] Pohl, II, p. 373.

[3] Köchel, 18. When the whole of Abel's Op. VII was published in 1767 by Bremner in London, the clarinet parts in No. 6 were given to oboes.

and Haydn's symphonies show very clearly how they wrote their scores to suit the resources of particulars orchestras. Disregarding the early symphony in E flat (K. 18), which was not his own composition, Mozart wrote clarinet parts in only four of his symphonies, and of these only two (K. 297 and K. 543) were originally scored for clarinets, and only one for both clarinets and oboes. This was the Paris symphony (K. 297) of 1778, written for the orchestra at the *Concert spirituel*, where he could rely on finding both instruments. To the other two (K. 385 and K. 550), the clarinet parts were added later for performances on occasions when these instruments were available.[1] Just in the same way, Haydn scored his symphonies to suit particular orchestras. When there were no clarinets in the orchestra at Esterház, these instruments are not in the scores; but when Haydn was writing for London he was able to include them. Gluck also, when he revised his Vienna operas for the Paris stage, wrote several clarinet parts which were not in the original Vienna scores.

Rather interesting is the association of clarinets with French horns which crops up repeatedly during the period when the former instrument was slowly but steadily gaining a footing in both orchestras and military bands. The first trace of this partnership seems to be the "overture," said to be in Handel's handwriting, for clarinets and horns, now preserved at Cambridge.[2] In the "London Public Advertiser" in 1754 it was announced: "By particular Desire, between the Acts, will be introduced several pieces for Clarinets and French horns," and in the same year a "Benefit" for "Mr. Solinus and Mr. Leander" was announced, with pieces for clarinets and horns between the acts.[3] Then in 1760 we find Arne using the same combination in "Thomas and Sally"; there, in Act I, scene 1, the instruments are used on the stage: "Half the following symphony is play'd behind the scenes at the further end. Then the Horns and Clarinets come on sounding the rest of the symphony, several huntsmen follow, and last of all, the Squire." In 1766 at Marylebone Gardens "Choice pieces on the Clarinets and French horns" were played by Messrs. Frickler, Henniz, Seipts and Rathyen,"[4] and later the same combination was heard at

---

[1] Jahn, II, pp. 201 and 209. The "Haffner" and the G Minor symphonies. To the "Haffner" Mozart *added* flute and clarinet parts, but in the case of the G Minor he re-wrote the oboe parts when adding the clarinet parts.

[2] Fitzwilliam Museum.   [3] See also, Pohl, I, p. 72, footnote 1.

[4] Newspaper announcements.

Ranelagh Gardens, Finch's Grotto Gardens[1] (1770), and at Vauxhall Gardens.[2]

In France there was clearly a similar alliance between the two instruments.[3] La Pouplinière brought both horns and clarinets into his orchestra about the same time, and in 1764 Valentin Roeser's *Essai d'instruction à l'usage de ceux qui composent pour la clarinette et le cor* was published in Paris. In 1772 Francœur wrote of *la Manière de travailler pour deux cors et deux clarinettes*,[4] and Procksch and Roeser both published pieces for this particular combination early in the 'seventies.

No doubt clarinets were found to be better partners for horns than were the oboes, and that it was already recognised that they were more effective than double-reeds in the open air is shown by the readiness with which they were being adopted by military bands while they were only rather slowly gaining ground in orchestras. Cucuel quotes the following written by Marc-François Beche in 1788: *C'est environ en l'année 1767 qu'on a fait servir des clarinettes à la chapelle du roi, ainsi que des cors de chasse. On a remarqué que dans ces susdits passages, les clarinettes faisoient meilleur effet que les hautbois.*[5]

Throughout the story of the introduction of the clarinet into the orchestra we find much of that same freedom of choice which permitted parts to be played by either flutes or oboes being extended to either clarinets or oboes. Conductors who now play music of the 18th century written up to about 1780 need not feel squeamish about interchanging the instruments when it is quite clear that the composers themselves had no such feelings on the subject. Many a small orchestra now can find two clarinets, but not two oboes; others which cannot provide two oboes can often find two flutes. If the change of tone-colour did not worry the composers of the music, it need not cause misgivings on the part of those who now play that music.

The composers of the generation of Arne, J. C. Bach, Abel, etc., wrote for a pair of oboes simply because these instruments were to be found in every orchestra; because they were accustomed to do so; it was their habit, and everyone else did so, and had done so before their time. It was not because the oboe produced just that particular shade of tone-colour for which their

[1] Wroth, pp. 204, 243, 244.   [2] *Ibid.*, p. 311.
[3] See Cucuel, *Études*, pp. 21 and 22; also *La Pouplinière*, pp. 390 and 393.
[4] *Traité général*, p. 51.   [5] *Études*, p. 21.

souls craved; not because their parts suited the oboe and no other instrument; and not because the double-reed instrument blended with the strings any better than other wind instruments.   It was a convention, and little else.   There are no oboe parts in all the earlier symphonies of Haydn or Mozart, or by any of that host of smaller fry who "also ran" in the 'fifties, 'sixties and 'seventies of the 18th century, that would not sound equally well if they were played on clarinets.   These composers would have written for clarinets had these instruments been available, and did write for them when they were available; they didn't seem to mind if the oboe parts were played on flutes.   Leopold Mozart offered some of his son's symphonies for "two violins, viola, two horns, *two oboes or transverse flutes* and double-bass" to Breitkopf in 1772.[1] Must we then suppose that because the old MS. or print says "oboes," that it must be oboes and nothing else?   Would these old composers turn in their graves if we change their conventional pair for something equally good?   No; the 19th century score may be rigid and dictatorial; it may make demands in its own inflexible way; but the old 18th century score or set of parts is much more easy-going, much more accommodating, and quite ready to adapt itself to varying circumstances.   A pair of wood-wind instruments in the soprano register is all it requires, and at a pinch it will cheerfully do without them if they cannot be found.[2]

When Mozart offered three piano concertos to the Paris publisher Sieber, he added, as an additional inducement, that they could be played with a full orchestra, or with oboes and horns, or with only a string quartet.[3]   In a performance of his "Entführung" at Salzburg the clarinet and cor anglais parts were played on violas,[4] and on another occasion he recommended that "should His Highness not have any clarinets at his court, a competent copyist might transpose the parts into suitable keys, in which case the first part should be played by a violin and the second by a viola."[5]   He knew better than to put obstacles in the way of getting his works played, and would readily alter the orchestration if there was any advantage to be gained by so doing.

[1] Letter, Feb. 7, 1772.

[2] In many of the old symphonics *all* the wind parts are *ad lib*: Dittersdorf, *Sinfonia nel gusto di cinque Nazioni, a quatro stromenti obbligati con due oboe e Corni da caccia ad libitum* (Paris, 1768).

[3] Letter, April 26, 1783.   [4] *Ibid.*, Nov. 28 (?), 1784.

[5] *Ibid.*, Sept. 30, 1786.

There could never be any difficulty on account of the compass
when oboe parts were transferred to the clarinet, for the latter
had an ample margin to spare at both ends of its scale.   Nor was
there likely to be much difficulty when the process was reversed,
because the early clarinet parts hardly touch the lower register
of the instrument, and in either case, if a transposition was
necessary, that was a perfectly simple matter.   As far as is known,
Mozart was the first to exploit the rich lower register of the
clarinet.

Such free-and-easy exchanges of instruments would, of course,
never do for the more mature orchestration of the 'eighties and
'nineties. But the pieces of that time are orchestrally on quite a
different plane from the earlier ones scored for only one pair of
treble wood-wind instruments.

When the flutes, oboes, clarinets and bassoons were made to
act side by side, when each was given its own function, and when
they were contrasted or blended and treated as four distinct
tone-colours, each taking its own share of the proceedings, a new
era in the history of orchestration was opened.   It is impossible
and always unwise to give any precise date for the beginning of
changes in musical history, for nothing happened suddenly; but
if a period must be named, it could be said that this new era
began during the last quarter of the 18th century, or probably
more exactly, during the last two decades of that century, when,
led by Mozart and followed up by Haydn, it dawned on composers that they had in their hands the material for instrumental
colouring such as had never been dreamed of hitherto.   Compare the wood-wind parts of the first Haydn symphony of 1759
and the childish Mozart first symphony of 1764 with those of the
sublime Mozart group of 1788 and Haydn's London symphonies
of 1791–94. In the earlier works the orchestration is hardly
conscious; it barely exists. In the later works it has come to
life, and is more than merely pointing the way for Beethoven,
Schubert and Weber, for a group of attentive French composers,
and for the alert Italians who were to take it up in the early 19th
century and fit it for further exploitation by Berlioz, Liszt and
Wagner.   The old man Haydn was quite right when he bemoaned
to Kalkbrenner: "I have only just learned in my old age how to
use the wind instruments, and now that I do understand them,
I must leave the world."

The horn and trumpet parts in the 18th century show a strong family likeness which is the natural result of the close relationship existing between the two instruments, a likeness which tended to make the parts almost indistinguishable, and even interchangeable. Both were originally open-air instruments endowed with a tone-weight far greater than that of any wood-wind or string instrument, and both were handicapped musically by the same imperfect scale. The occasions for their use were very much the same, and, like the style of the parts written for them, they fall historically into two categories, the periods of which correspond roughly to the two halves of the century.

The scores of the earlier period show how horns and trumpets were employed on selected occasions to play parts which were melodically conceived; whereas in the later period these instruments were used on ordinary occasions, and the parts lose most of their melodic character.

In the earlier period both instruments were treated as the more noisy element in orchestration. The parts written for them, therefore, occur mostly in works designed for performance in spacious places—in Masses, oratorios and church music generally, also in opera and theatrical music, but not so often in purely instrumental music intended for the smaller chamber or concert-room. As Schubart wrote: "The trumpet can be used by composers only on big, festive and majestic occasions."[1]

It might be that the association of the trumpet with the battle-field, or of the horn with the hunting-field, would sometimes bring about the appearance of one or other of these instruments in the scores of vocal works when the words invited some such appropriate or realistic colouring; but, on the whole, these instruments were employed largely for the sake of the volume of sound which they could contribute to the music, for the sake of their brilliance and the stimulating energy with which they could endow the *ensemble* and give it the effect of eventfulness or climax. Their use in the scores of the earlier period is always in the nature of a special event, a high light in the proceedings, rather than as an occurrence in the ordinary course of orchestration. Thus, it may be in only three or four numbers of an oratorio or opera that any brass parts are found; perhaps in two or three big choruses, perhaps in a big instrumental movement, or possibly as a solo *obbligato* in an aria. The horns or trumpets might be employed separately, both together, or not at all. One

[1] Schubart, p. 197.

cannot count on finding parts for them in every score, nor in every fully-scored movement, nor at every *fortissimo*. What they contribute to the sound of the music is reserved for occasions which lie outside of the ordinary everyday events of orchestration.

In the scores of the later period the horn and trumpets parts occur, not so much as a special event, but as a matter of course whenever the quantity of sound is to be increased. They lend their weight and colour, not to a few specially selected moments, but to all fully-scored movements, or at any moment when a full volume of sound is required. The addition of brass tone occurs, so to speak, automatically, whenever the dynamics of the music rise above a certain level. Thus, in the later 18th century scores, horn parts are to be found in almost every work, be it opera, oratorio, symphony or overture, and in all except the lightly-scored or quiet movements. Trumpet and drum parts similarly occur fairly regularly and as a matter of course, but then they are generally reserved for the quicker and heavier movements.

In all 18th century scores, early or late, except when one trumpet is used as a solo *obbligato* instrument, drums go hand in hand with trumpets in their traditional role as the bass instrument of the group. If in the earlier scores a drum part does not always appear with that of the trumpets, that is no good reason for concluding that drums were not intended to be used. The parts were of a standard type which could easily be improvised or played from a trumpet part by anyone who was familiar with the conventions of the drummer's art. The drum parts were not always or necessarily written out in the score, and sometimes they are admitted only as if they were rather grudged the space they occupy.[1] Although there may be no evidence to support the suggestion, it might be surmised that it was not an uncommon custom to leave the drum part to the drummer's invention, or possibly to write out a part for him without troubling to include it in the written score.

The melodic horn and trumpet parts written in the first half of the 18th century were the outcome of attempts to make instruments with an imperfect scale take part in music which was contrapuntally conceived, and which, therefore, could find no place in its texture for non-melodic parts. The unmechanised horns and trumpets of that time, on which only the notes of the

---

[1] Sometimes noted on the same stave as the trumpets, or in the bass part.

natural harmonic series could be sounded, were obviously useless
for melodic purposes in their two lower octaves; in the third
octave they could sound only the arpeggio on the common
chord, and not till the fourth octave was reached could the
consecutive notes of a diatonic scale be produced, and then only
with increasing difficulty and uncertainty as the scale rose
towards the 16th open note.   In endeavouring to preserve the
melodic character of the parts, the composers were obliged to
keep them in the 3rd and 4th octaves of the harmonic series, and
to keep them in the higher octave as much as possible in order to
be able to take advantage of the scale-wise order of the sounds.
They were really trying to make horns and trumpets play the
same sort of parts as they wrote for violins and oboes; they
modified the brass parts only when obliged to do so owing to the
lack of consecutive sounds in the third octave of the harmonic
series.

Example II.   HANDEL, DETTINGEN TE DEUM

It is not at all uncommon to find the horns and trumpets
sharing the same part in the scores of this period.   Occasionally

one is invited either to choose between the two instruments[1] or
to use them both together.   Even when no choice is specifically
indicated we may suspect that in such cases the omission of
one or other of them would not seriously offend the spirit
of the departed composer nor in any way diminish the good
effect.

The melodic and florid parts played in the open notes of
natural horns and trumpets gradually gave way round about
the middle of the 18th century to a type of part which was
largely non-melodic and lay more in the medium register of the
instruments.

As a reason for this change in the manner of writing for horns
and trumpets it has often been said that composers ceased to
write that sort of part because that particular style of playing
declined and died out in the second half of the century.   But why
should it have died out?   Why should players have lost their
command of the highest register of the instruments just at that
particular time, when players on all other instruments were
steadily increasing their executive skill?   There can have been
only one reason; and that was because composers no longer
wrote that sort of part.   The old style of playing declined
simply because there was no longer any demand for it.   And
if it is asked why composers ceased to write in the old style,
again, there can be only one answer: because they didn't like it.
If they had wished to continue writing in that style there was
nothing to prevent them doing so; and if they had done so, the
old style of playing would not have declined and died out.
With a growing sense for fitness in orchestration, musicians
would have no more of these screaming trumpets and hiccuping
horns in their music.   The old style of part had never really
suited the instruments; the parts had always been difficult and
uncertain; the playing involved strain on the part of both
players[2] and listeners; and in the fourth octave of the harmonic
series at least two notes were rather badly out of tune.   There
was nothing to be said for the old style of part, and orchestration
lost nothing good when it was abandoned.   All that the old high

[1] "Six Select Symphonies for two violins, two trumpets or French horns, a tenor
obbligato, violoncello and basso figured for the Harpsichord" (From a London
title-page).

[2] A virtuoso trumpeter named Gräf while playing at a concert died from
hæmorrhage of the lungs brought on by excessive exertion (Schubart, p. 125).

florid trumpet and horn parts left behind them was a legacy of trouble whenever the old works were revived.

The new style of part fitted well into the texture of music which was made up more of melody and accompanying harmony, and less of contrapuntal strands. The horns and trumpets were given sustained notes and rhythmical patterns in the upper, medium and lower registers, where they could be played with reasonable safety, and unobtrusively when it was desired. The extreme high register was left alone. The rather grotesque capering about under difficulties in the highest register was ruled out, and a more dignified if less exacting function was allotted to the heaviest voices of the orchestra.

Simultaneously with the advent of the new sort of part there developed a new style of horn-playing. The instrument was held at the player's side, and his hand was placed in the bell. This manner of playing gave him not only some additional sounds, but it mellowed the quality of the sound and developed a quieter and more pleasant tone, the dreamy, velvety quality which is the main charm of horn-tone. Horn parts were then written in all sorts of works and in all sorts of movements; not only on special occasions and not only for rather noisy effects, but as a normal procedure in the ordinary course of orchestration. In the symphonies and overtures of the 'sixties and 'seventies the horns played in the first and last movements as a matter of course, and soon began to find their way into the minuets and slow movements. In the opera scores too, horn parts occur commonly as part and parcel of the normal orchestration. Playing a horn part was no longer a *tour de force*, demanding a specially qualified player braced up for a special effort.

Whereas the old style of horn part was an essential part of the music, having melodic-thematic interest of its own, the function of the new style of part was rather to give body and cohesion to the ensemble. It filled out the inner harmonic structure, and was less concerned with melodic outlines. The parts are therefore uneventful, and musically rather dull; but they supplied what the orchestra had previously lacked, namely, a more substantial and better balanced volume of sound in the middle register. The nature of these horn parts is reflected in the words which often appear on the title-pages of the printed parts of many old symphonies: "les Cors de chasse ad lib."[1]   The essentials of the music were all contained in the string parts; the horns supplied additional volume, colour and cohesion, but could be omitted if the instruments were not available.

Although stopping was generally practised by all solo horn players during the last quarter of the century, the ordinary orchestral parts rarely demand any but the open notes, keeping, on the whole, within the range from (written) g to g″.   For solo parts, of course, much more was demanded, and in the concertos written for the famous horn virtuosi of the 'eighties and 'nineties the solo parts are florid and exacting.

The trumpet parts written after the old melodic and florid style of writing had been abandoned are very like the contemporary horn parts in that they have hardly any melodic movement. Trumpets and drums, however, were generally reserved for the loudest moments of the orchestration, and the parts are consequently neither so many nor so long as the horn parts.   In the ordinary course a composer wrote trumpet and drum parts in the first and last movements of a symphony, and in the choruses and finales of an opera, and then only when the fullest power of the orchestra was required.   In a dramatic work an occasional flourish or military call might bring these instruments to the front when the situation demanded some martial flavouring, but apart from such special occasions the trumpets and drums were used only to give greater volume and brilliance to the orchestral ensemble.   Like the horn parts, the trumpet parts were not usually an essential part of the musical structure, and could be omitted without depriving the music of anything but volume and colour.

The old contemporary sets of parts supply evidence which supports the conjecture that trumpets and drums were very often treated as unessential instruments which might be added to or omitted from a score just as circumstances allowed.   A symphony by Joh. Stamitz, for example, was published in Paris by Huberty with trumpet and drum parts, while a contemporary London edition is without these parts.   Another symphony by the same composer[2] was published in Paris with parts for only strings and horns; but two MS. sets of parts

---

[1] The horn parts of a symphony by Gossec (1759) were sold separately—*on vens les cors de chasse séparément.*

[2] Op. III, No. 2.

exist[1] in which there are also parts for oboes, trumpets and drums. The title of three symphonies by Gossec, Haydn and Bach (J. C.), published in Paris about 1773, includes the words: *avec timbales et trompettes qui se vendent séparément*; obviously, one could play them with or without these instruments. Similar cases of symphonies by Filtz, Toeschi, Cannabich, Gossec and Carl Stamitz occur in which one set of parts includes trumpet and drum parts, while another is without them. It is significant that it is often a MS. set that contains the additional parts, a circumstance which suggests that the reduced instrumentation was a publisher's device designed to save expense in engraving, and at the same time to widen the field for the sale of the music. While this undoubtedly was the case, such things cannot always have been done without the connivance of the composer, and we have ample reason to suppose that composers were not unwilling to adapt the instrumentation of their works to suit local conditions and resources.

We know that Mozart added parts to some of his orchestral works, and that he did so on separate sheets of paper without embodying them in the score. We owe our knowledge of these parts only to the accident that certain bits of paper have survived and have been found. But such things are easily lost, and who can tell how many such parts have been destroyed in the critical period after a composer's death when his MSS. and copied parts are often reckoned of little or no value. There is, in all probability, not one of the hundreds of published symphonies written in the second half of the 18th century for which the composer either did not write trumpet and drum parts, or would not have been quite ready to do so had there been any occasion for their use. One wonders if some or all of the Haydn and Mozart symphonies now published in the Complete editions for strings, oboes and horns, had not at some time or other trumpet and drum parts as well. That such parts do not appear in the autograph scores is no guarantee that they never existed.

The notation used for horns and trumpets in the old scores varies considerably. In addition to the ordinary transposing notation which was standardised in the 19th century, the parts are sometimes written at their actual pitch for trumpets, and an octave above the real sounds for horns. Another notation for

---

[1] At Regensburg and in the author's collection. In the latter case the work is ascribed to Carl Stamitz. This symphony with the full orchestration is reprinted in the *Denkmäler Deutscher Tonkunst* series.

horns is not uncommon. This is so contrived that when the part is read with the treble clef it gives the correct transposed notation for the player, but when it is read with another clef it gives the real sounds, either at their actual pitch or an octave too low, for the benefit of the score-reader. If, for example, the movement is in E flat, then the bass clef is used, because the note C in the treble stave becomes E when the bass clef is substituted. In this case, of course, the notes are an octave below the real sounds. Similarly, if the piece was in D, the alto clef would be used, and the notes would then be at the correct pitch.[1] The disadvantages of this system were, that in some cases the real sounds were given an octave too low, and also that when the eleventh open note of the horn's natural scale was used as a (written) F sharp, the accidental was incorrect in keys with flats in the key-signature.[2]

The violin parts in 18th century scores show that the players were not expected to play in any position higher than the third, at any rate, for the greater part of that period. Towards the end of the century, however, the violin parts creep up to f''' fairly freely, and occasionally even up to g'''.[3] .

In the earlier scores the parts for first and second violins generally move, when not playing in unison, in a duet-like partnership, rather close together, and not infrequently crossing one another. There is much unison playing, but even when the parts are independent they share very much the same matter, it may be fugally, imitatively, or in parallel thirds or sixths. The parts are technically easy according to present standards, but the spare orchestration of that time leaves nothing to the imagination; every note is heard, and the playing is therefore submitted to a searching test which readily exposes any flaws in the execution and the *ensemble*. Quantz remarked on a considerable increase in the technical difficulty of orchestral parts during his lifetime, and asserted that the *ripieno* parts were then (1752) often more exacting than the solo parts of the early 18th century.[4]

In the later 18th century violin parts there is less of the patterned violin-figuration of the old Italian school, and much more harmonic and accompanying figuration. The changing style of the

[1] For examples in musical notation, see Carse, *History of Orchestration*, p. 115.

[2] Similar notation was sometimes used for clarinets. Bach's *Orione* overture, for example.

[3] Beethoven would never take his first violins above a'''.

[4] *Versuch*, XVII, par. 3.

music brought into being matter which was harmonically rather than contrapuntally conceived, and the violins therefore got, in addition to melody and passage-work, a considerable share of the reiterated quavers or semiquavers which were such important ingredients of the new style. So, instead of always playing the principal melodic line, the violins had to put up with a certain amount of secondary matter or harmonic padding which is less interesting to play, but which served to build up a number of new orchestral textures, all of which, in their turn, became commonplaces long before the end of the century.

When in their original condition, most 18th century violin parts are plentifully sprinkled with shakes and the small ornamental notes which, no doubt, were quite well understood in their time. The exact interpretation of these small notes has become very uncertain during the passage of time, and has caused much trouble to 19th century editors, who have sometimes interpreted them according to their own ideas, and at other times have generously passed on these little problems to the conductors who eventually have to deal with them.

One thing which even the original copies of 18th century music cannot restore to us is the free and unwritten embellishments with which every violinist or soloist of "taste" was expected to embroider any sustained and *cantabile* melody. The theoretical works and instruction books make it only too clear that no simple sustained melodic part was played exactly as it was written; it had to be adorned with more or less elaborate ornamental figures which conformed to the harmony but which sometimes distorted the melodic outline almost beyond recognition. For examples of how this was done the reader is referred to the old theoretical works.[1] While, to us, it is almost inconceivable that such things were ever done, there can be no doubt about it; they were done. The arbitrary embellishment of simple melodies is now happily a neglected if not a lost art, and there seems to be no good reason why it should ever be revived;[2] but it is a thing which would have to be reckoned with if any attempt were made to reconstruct the rendering of 18th century music exactly as it was in its own time.

[1] Leopold Mozart, Chap. XI, pars. 17 to 22; Marpurg, *Anleitung z. Klavierspielen* (1755); and especially, Quantz, *Versuch*, XIII, *Von den willkührlichen Veränderungen über die simpeln Intervalle.* For examples, see Tables XVII, XVIII, XIX in Quantz.

[2] It has its modern counterpart in the way dance band players now freely elaborate their parts. ' "Swing it!"

Of all the instruments in the orchestra none was treated so shabbily by 18th century composers as was the viola. The viola part was at its best when a skilled composer wrote contrapuntally in four parts for strings, and let the viola take full responsibility for one of them. But, either few composers had that skill, or if they had they didn't exercise it, for a good viola part is the exception rather than the rule in 18th century scores. Even Handel, who could handle four or more choral parts with the greatest of ease, gave his violas the most undistinguished part in the score; sometimes he ignored them altogether; or he switched them on to play the bass part an octave higher, or gave them a part made up of the notes of the triads which were not required at the moment by the violins or in the bass part. Perhaps the clue to this unkind treatment may be found in the remarks with which Quantz introduces his essay on the duties of the viola player. Himself a conscientious musician, Quantz gave it as his opinion that the viola player ought to be every bit as good a musician as the second violin player, but he made it clear that as a rule he was not: "The viola is commonly regarded as a thing of little consequence in music. This may be because the instrument is generally played either by beginners or by those who have no particular talent for playing the violin, or perhaps because it is unprofitable to the player; therefore, able musicians are not at all anxious to play it."[1] They had no pride, these viola players. Quantz considered that they were not industrious enough. Many of them, he wrote, thought that if they knew a little about time and note-values, that was as much as could be expected of them. It was all their own fault. If they would only work harder they might improve their position instead of remaining mere viola players to the end of their days, as most of them did. Quantz went on to say that the viola player must on no account add any embellishments of his own to the written part. Perhaps, if he had been allowed to do so, he would have taken more interest in life, and might have overcome his inferiority complex.

But it was obviously a case of the vicious circle; composers wrote poor parts for the viola because the instrument was not well played, and it was not well played because composers wrote such poor parts for it.

If the viola parts in the first half of the century were dull, those

[1] *Versuch*, XVII, Part III, par. 1.

of the 'sixties and 'seventies were certainly no better. In the symphonies of that period, when it does not double a bass part which itself is none too interesting,[1] the viola part is a dreary waste of repeated quavers and semiquavers. All the harmonic drudgery of the orchestra went to the viola, and if some scrap of melodic movement did chance to come its way, the part was always doubled by some other instrument. Even in the 'eighties and 'nineties the viola was rarely given any independent melodic movement of its own. It was still made to hang on to the bass part; it had to share any little bit of fat in the tenor register with the 'cellos, or else it had to saw away at the harmonic padding which occupies so much of the gap between the violin and the bass parts. Mozart and Haydn, in their last and best symphonies, occasionally let it have a little true independence, but neither could get away from the tradition that this Cinderella of the orchestra must either cling to the bass part or just supply the note of the chord which the violins and the basses didn't want. In the last movement of Mozart's Jupiter Symphony the part-writing is sometimes such that it splits the string orchestra into five independent melodic parts, and then the viola *must* have one of them all to itself. But there was only one Jupiter Symphony, and only one movement like that last one in the whole of the 18th century.

That the viola never received fair treatment during the 18th century may also be traced to the way composers laid out their string parts in the first half of the century. They relied very much on the harmony supplied by the keyboard-instrument, and did not generally take the trouble to lay out the string parts in four-part harmony of which the viola would normally take the responsibility for the tenor part. Probably because they could get over the ground quickly, perhaps because it was the accepted custom, or possibly because they were uncritical of orchestral effect, composers were only too often content with a three-part lay-out for strings, which might be either of the following:

(*a*) two violin and a bass part;
(*b*) the same with violas doubling the bass in octaves;
(*c*) violins in unison, violas and the bass part.

Unless the parts are very carefully written (and it cannot be said

---

[1] The dull bass parts consisting largely of repeated quavers were known in Germany as *Trommelbässe*, i.e. drum-basses (see C. P. E. Bach, I, *Einleitung*, par. 7).

of most 18th century composers that they exercised any great
care in part-writing) all of the above lack body; the chords could
not all be complete, and what was lacking was left to the keyboard-instrument to supply.   The balance of tone, already none
too good in the case of (*b*) and (*c*), was often made worse by the
addition of oboes to the top part and bassoons to the bass part;
the viola part in (*c*) was never reinforced by a wind part because
there was no wind instrument then in general use with a compass
corresponding to that of the viola.   There was really little to be
said in favour of these three-part arrangements for strings except
that they could be written easily and quickly.   Speed and ease,
however, were important considerations in the days when composers turned out work after work in quick succession; they
could not labour long at each work, and the scores often show all
the signs of haste.   These three-part string groups were the
rough and ready methods of a period when the aim was quantity
rather than quality, and when ears were not very sensitive to the
niceties of balance and blend in orchestration.

When a composer turned on the violas to play the bass part in
octaves, it was not because that part was in any great need of
reinforcement; it was a labour-saving device, a ready way of
saving himself the trouble of thinking out the music in four parts.
He had only to write a few words in the score or say a word or
two to the copyist, and the viola part was finished.   He might
not even take the trouble to see how it worked out; and if the
violas did chance to get above the violin parts or clashed with the
melody, it could easily be put right when the piece was played.
It is difficult to believe that Handel really intended his violas
to behave as they do in the following examples:

Example III.   HANDEL, "ESTHER"

Quantz warned the viola player that he must never play above
the top part of the music, and seemed to think, rather unfairly,

that it was the responsibility of the player to see that such a thing did not occur. It was not the composer, but the wretched player who had to decide when his part threatened to get out of bounds and was going to overleap the melody. Leopold Mozart remarked[1] that this sort of thing (allowing the bass to get above the uppermost part) was a common fault amongst half-composers (*halbcomponisten*). Alas! "whole composers" were also occasional defaulters.

The habit of thinking out the string music in three parts was one which 18th century composers never quite got rid of. There is still much of it in the later works of Haydn and Mozart, and it can be traced even in the way Beethoven laid out his string parts.

It was only towards the end of the century that the bass part in the full score ceased to be a bass part in general, and began to be split into separate parts, each of which was designed for a specific instrument. It was then that the 'cello, the double-bass and the bassoon parts began to go each their own way, and could be recognised as having characteristics of their own and functions which they did not necessarily share among them. The lowest stave in the score then ceases to be only "basso"; it becomes "violoncello e basso," the latter word designating the actual instrument, the string double-bass, and not only the bass part of the music. The figuring also disappears, and tells of the waning influence of the keyboard-instrument in the orchestra; the bassoons find a stave higher up in the score, and link themselves up with the growing wood-wind group as their particular bass voice.

Various niceties of orchestration begin to appear in these lower parts; little things which were hardly recognised as long as there was only one universal bass part. The difference between the 8-foot bass of the 'cello and the 16-foot bass of the double-bass is more and more exploited; the latter is silenced for a little, and then joins in again with all the greater effect. The *pizzicato* of the lower string instruments lends lightness and variety of colour to the bass part. The bassoons are given sustained sounds instead of the reiteration which is native to bowed string instruments but not to wind instruments. Perhaps the greatest of all was the discovery that so much could be made of the rich and telling tone on the A string of the 'cello in the capacity of

[1] *Einleitung*, par. 2.

melodist or counter-melodist. This opened up a new field for
melodic parts in the tenor register of the orchestra, which, even
if it was only tentatively exploited in the 18th century, was the
beginning of the independent 'cello parts which figure so
prominently in 19th century scores.

The editor or arranger of 18th century scores is often faced
with problems which cannot always be authoritatively settled.
He must either make up his own mind about them, or else hand
on his difficulties to the performer or conductor.

The interpretation of the small ornamental notes which
abound in most 18th century scores has already been mentioned,
and is an ever-present problem. It should not be supposed that
there is any lack of contemporary information on this subject.
On the contrary, more than enough of it may be found in numbers
of theoretical works and instruction books.[1] Ornamentation,
indeed, was reckoned a most important feature of both singing
and playing, and the amount of space devoted to the rendering
of shakes and ornaments in the 18th century tutors seems, to our
view, disproportionately large. In the important foreign tutors
a whole chapter or more is generally given to instructing the
pupil how to interpret the signs and little notes which are so
plentifully scattered about the old music pages, or how to add
them if they are not already there. The short English tutors,
while they skim over the whole technique of an instrument in
three or four pages, never omit a table of shakes and list of
"graces."[2] It might be imagined that, with such copious en-
lightenment, there need never be any question of how this or
that small note should be rendered. Yet, with the best will in the
world, it is often difficult or impossible to apply to particular cases
the precepts so plentifully supplied, and it is not at all unlikely
that the enquirer may find himself more bewildered after consulting the old authorities than before seeking their aid.

The following are some of the causes of uncertainty: for every
rule that is laid down there is always a number of exceptions,
and it may not be clear whether a rule or one of its exceptions
applies to a particular case; the explanations are not always clear,
and sometimes appear to be contradictory; all authorities do not

---

[1] Türk, Marpurg, Agricola, Quantz, Rousseau, Leopold Mozart, Koch, etc., etc.

[2] According to the late 18th century English tutors, "God save the King"
should never be played without a shake on every dotted crotchet.

always agree;[1] there are differences in the styles and names of ornaments in different countries—in Italy, Germany or France.

Most of the difficulties lie in the fact that the 18th century writers had no standard way of distinguishing between the notation of a long *appoggiatura*, which has a definite time-value, and a short one (now called *acciaccatura*), which has hardly any perceptible time-value; and also because apparently almost any note-value might be used for an *appoggiatura* without relation to the value of the main note. The whole matter became much clearer when a little diagonal stroke was drawn across the tail of the short *acciaccatura*; but that device appears to have been unknown for the greater part of the 18th century. Even now, when the signs or notation have become more or less standardised, the *appoggiatura* is often diversely interpreted, and, if it matters less in solo parts, any divergence in orchestral parts is not unimportant.

The absence of any indication of *tempo* in an old score is a matter which an editor usually deals with, and his judgment is handed on, for better or for worse, to the conductor, who will make a final adjustment according to his judgment. Between them, who can say how far they may have strayed from the composer's intentions? Even when the *tempo* is stated, it is not always clear to which unit of the time-signature it applies. This is sometimes in doubt when the *Alla-breve* time-signature is used. If the composer wrote *Allegro vivace*, *Allegro molto*, *Presto*, or some such words, we know that he meant the movement to be played at a quick speed, but the question may arise: is it the crotchet or the minim rate which is to be quick? Again, in *Andante* movements in two-four time, there may be doubt as to whether it is the crotchet or the quaver which is to move at the *Andante* pace. In such cases the value of the shortest notes employed will give some guidance as to the *tempo*; in the end it is the nature of the music itself on which judgment will probably be based, but it must be admitted that the *tempo* which seems just right to one may seem wrong to another. As no notation or *tempo* marks are proof against misunderstanding, a movement, in the course of its progress from 18th century composer to 20th century conductor, may undergo some strange changes of *tempo*.

[1] This is especially the case when the question arises whether a short ornamental note should fall *on* or *before* the accent.

The scarcity or absence of any indications of *piano*, *forte*, and marks of expression in the old scores may raise problems which can hardly be ignored when the old works are revived. Contemporary scores and parts *may* make a distinction between loud and soft, and they often do so; the effect of a soft phrase echoing a loud one was a favourite device with the earlier 18th century composers, and the rhythmical construction of the music or even the orchestration may be helpful in restoring to the right places any such effects which are not clearly marked. But the shades of tone-quantity between the loud and the soft, also indications that the change was to be anything but sudden, are usually absent till about the middle of the century, when they begin to appear tentatively in the MS. and printed parts. There is a wide field for speculation on this subject. Did the earlier composers require anything more than alternations of loud and soft when their works were played, or did they rely on the instinct, taste and musicianship of their executants, or on customs or understandings of which we know nothing, for the finer shades of tone-gradation? It would be mere guess-work to attempt to answer such questions. As far as the older scores and parts are concerned, perfunctory indications of either *forte* or *piano* playing are all that we have to guide us, and if these are to be interpreted exactly as they stand on paper, then nothing more was required. Yet it is absurd to suppose that the musicians of that time knew nothing of the finer tone-gradations which were certainly at their command if they had chosen to make use of them, or that they were insensitive to the effects of increasing or diminishing tone-quantities which their instruments and voices were always capable of supplying.[1] Tradition, custom, and their own verbal instructions no doubt provided much that the written pages do not reveal; but whether they did or not, it is a fact that the earlier composers took very little trouble to make their intentions clear on paper.

The 18th century theorists give the impression that it was expected of good musicians to know how and when to vary the dynamics of their playing to suit the situation without having it all clearly set out in their parts. Because there is no indication of loud or soft in an old score, it need not be assumed that no such gradations of tone were desired, or that the performer is

[1] See Leopold Mozart, Chap. I, sec. 3; C. P. E. Bach, Book I, Chap. III, par. 29; Quantz, Chap. XI, par. 14, and Chap. XIV, pars. 9, 10, 11.

F

strictly carrying out the intentions of the composer when he plays with unvarying tone-quantity throughout a whole movement.   It is much more likely that he is disregarding the intentions of the composer, who considered it quite unnecessary to provide leading-strings for competent musicians.

The later 18th century scores are provided with more specific indications of dynamic light and shade.   In the 'fifties, 'sixties and 'seventies, a distinction between *forte* and *fortissimo*, or between *piano* and *pianissimo*, is often made; *mezzoforte* and *mezzo piano*, also the various signs and expressions corresponding to *crescendo* and *diminuendo* begin to appear.   Gluck's printed scores are fairly fully marked, and in the printed parts of the numerous symphonies published during these three decades there are directions which show that composers were, even if not very careful in marking their music, at any rate making use of a number of tone-gradations other than only loud and soft.   By the end of the century most of the conventional signs now in use had become standardised, and composers indicated with some precision the usual tone-gradations from *pianissimo* to *fortissimo*, the *sforzando* and other accents, without, however, attempting to specify the finer nuances with which modern scores are so plentifully supplied.

A feature of the notation in 18th century scores and parts which ought to be faced, but which is generally shirked by both editors and conductors, is the uncertain value of the dotted note. The general rule that the dot increased the value of a note by half as much again certainly applied to crotchets and all longer notes, but not to quavers and notes of less time-value.   The note which followed the dot was delayed until the last moment, thus giving the effect, in all but quick *tempi*, of a double-dotted or even a triple-dotted note.   The words of contemporary theorists are unequivocal, and they must be believed.   C. P. E. Bach, Leopold Mozart and Quantz all draw attention to the uncertain value of the dot, and make it quite clear that in slow movements the dotted quaver was played as if it were double-dotted.   C. P. E. Bach puts it as follows: "The short notes which follow dotted notes are always played shorter than they are written."[1]   And again: "The manner of writing dotted notes is often very inaccurate.   It is therefore advisable to lay down a general rule for the rendering of such notes, even though it is subject to many

[1] Bach, Book I, Chap. III, par. 23.

exceptions. *The notes following dotted notes should be played as short as possible.*"[1] Quantz explains quite clearly that the dotted minim and dotted crotchet are worth, respectively, three crotchets and three quavers, but that quavers and shorter notes do not conform to the same rule. Quantz, Bach and L. Mozart each give illustrations which show how the short note was delayed till the last moment:[2]

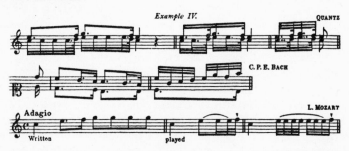

Leopold Mozart explains that in certain slow passages the value of the dot must be increased in order to prevent the performance becoming sleepy: "if the dot is held for its usual length, the music sounds very lazy and sleepy."[3] Mozart's father is some-times credited with the invention of the double dot: "It would be a good thing if the duration of the dot could be quite definitely established. I, at any rate, have often done this, and have shown my meaning by using two dots, with a corresponding shortening of the succeeding note. It is true, it looks strange. But what does that matter?"[4]

Prolonging the dotted note and shortening the note after it in the manner described above would, of course, have no appre-ciable effect when the *tempo* was quick, and very little when it was moderate; but the difference of the effect in the case of slowish or slow *tempi* would be very considerable, and might alter the whole character of the music. The dotted note was a characteristic of the slow introductory movement which preceded the fugal *Allegro* in overtures written on the Lullian model, and the old rule should certainly be applied to the many works written in that style, at all events, up to about the 'sixties or 'seventies of the 18th

[1] Bach, Book II, Chap. XXIX, par. 15.

[2] Quantz, *Versuch*, Chap. V, pars. 20, 21, 22, 23.

[3] Mozart, *Versuch*, Chap. I, Sec. 3, par. 11. See also, Chap. IV, pars. 11, 12, 13, and Chap. IX, par. 4.

[4] *Ibid.*, Chap. I, Sec. 3, par. 11.

century. It would apply to many of Handel's overtures, and to the first movements (overtures) of J. S. Bach's orchestral suites.

By using the double and even the triple dot, the later composers did away with the ambiguity which surrounded the duration of the single dot. While we may be quite certain that composers did adopt the present system of dotting notes during the last two or three decades of the century, thus making their intentions quite clear, it is equally certain that the works of their predecessors are being misinterpreted when they are played without taking into consideration the earlier custom of prolonging the dotted quaver until almost the very end of the beat.

At the end of the century, although the present system was by then pretty well standardised, it is evident that the old interpretation of the dot still lingered. In Koch's *Lexikon* (1802), two cases are cited in music type to show when the old rule still applied.[1] That the old rule was not peculiar to Germany only, and that it also held good in this country, is suggested by the following from a flute tutor published in London as late as 1794:

Example V.

"In all the examples hitherto given, it is to be observed, that the point (dot) is added to a note which is the common measure (beat), and consequently what is added to it, belongs to another measure (beat) or accented part of the bar; the short note next after the point (dot) together with it, making up that measure (beat); but it is done by the present practice in such a manner, as to give the dot by far the greatest part of that measure (beat), and leaving the smallest remainder possible for the short note following, which may be considered as a very short connective particle at the end of the second measure (beat), pronounced as near as possible to the third. . . . But when the dot is added to a character (note) which is less than a measure (beat) of the bar, it must be included in the time of such measure (beat), in such a manner as to give the pointed (dotted) note almost the whole of it, and consequently the note after the dot made as short as

[1] Koch, *Lexikon*, Art. *Punct.*

possible, just slipt in before the following note, which will be an accented one."[1]

It should be understood that the same treatment was given to a short accented note preceding a dotted note. This, the "Scotch snap," was a very common rhythmical characteristic in the instrumental music of the 18th century, and if it is to be correctly interpreted, the short accented note should be made as short as possible.

Although less frequent, there are a few other problems which are always liable to confront anyone who seeks to bring to light the forgotten orchestral music of the 18th century. There may be doubt, for example, whether the composer intended quickly reiterated notes in the string parts to be played strictly according to their written value or as an unmeasured *tremolo*. In the case of both quick and slow movements, when semi-quavers are repeated, there can be little doubt that they were meant to be played as semiquavers, and that no *tremolo* was intended. The use of reiterated demisemiquavers may raise some doubts, and cases occur which might be interpreted either way. The real unmeasured bow-tremolo, however, is more a 19th century than an 18th century orchestral texture, and it may be questioned whether 18th century composers ever made use of it, at any rate, till rather late in the century.

A wavy or zigzagged line, which may be found in many contemporary scores and parts of the 18th century, presents a problem which has never been completely solved. It appears commonly in the string parts, over or under repeated demisemiquavers, semiquavers, quavers or crotchets, and sometimes over long sustained notes. It is generally supposed to have indicated a sort of *tremolo* bowing, the exact nature of which is not known.[2] In Kastner's *Traité Général d'Instrumentation* (1836)[3] it is explained as follows: *Les sons ondulés: C'est un coup d'archet qu'on indique par les signes ～～～ et qui consiste dans plusiers sons filés, dont on fait sentir le forté au commencement de chaque tems ou de chaque demi-tems de la mesure.*

Example VI.

[1] John Gunn, The School of the German Flute, p. 10.
[2] Forsyth, p. 350.   [3] Kastner, p. 7.

That this sign indicated a variety of bowing seems quite certain, but that explanation does not account for the fact that it may also be found in a few parts for wind instruments.[1]

The question whether a part was to be played by a single wind instrument or by several, may possibly arise in the earlier scores. The use of oboes and bassoons as *ripieno*-instruments was then very general, and there can be little doubt that except when the part assumes the character of a leading solo, or in *obbligati* to vocal solos, it was meant to be played by all available instruments in chorus.

Mistakes of all sorts are plentiful enough in the old original 18th century scores and parts, both MS. and printed. When these are obviously copyist's or engraver's errors they are generally corrected, and no more is said about them. When similar errors occur in composer's autograph MSS. there seems to be no good reason why these too should not be put right. But when the composer belongs to the category now called "great," he is apt to be regarded as infallible, as one who could not make a mistake, and the error is perpetuated just because HE wrote it with HIS own hands. Actually, of course, he was just as liable to make mistakes in writing as was the lesser man, and it seems unfair that his slips of the pen should cause him to be misrepresented just because his music was of better quality than that of his contemporaries. After all, the great man's greatness does not lie in the accuracy of his musical calligraphy; like the rest of them, he wrote much and quickly; he did not know that future generations were going to treasure every note he put down on paper and treat it as something sacred, unalterable, beyond dispute and everlastingly final.

Once an error creeps into the first printed edition of a "classic," it seems to be there for ever. True, the great man may never have seen a proof sheet; the piece may have been published without his consent, or after his death; but next to the original MS., the First Edition is sacrosanct, authoritative and inviolable; let no mere editor dare to lay his insignificant hands on the great man's thoughts—or his mistakes.

---

[1] In oboe parts by Gluck and Arne.

Chapter VI

CONCLUSION. ARRANGEMENTS. STANDARD OF
PERFORMANCE

The matter set forth in the previous chapter may help to provide answers to such questions as are sometimes asked: Why cannot 18th century music be played just as it was written? Why is it so often edited by So-and-So or arranged by Such-and-Such? The whole question of how to perform 18th century orchestral music under present conditions opens up a wide field for discussion. The earlier the music, the greater are the problems, and the more controversial any views which may be expressed.

On the whole, it may be stated, without fear of contradiction, that late 18th century orchestral music requires no arranging, no re-orchestrating, and very little editing. A few inconsistencies in the bowing, phrasing or articulation are sure to be found in the original scores, and some obvious errors or misprints may be discovered. These are easily put right; but the music and the orchestration remain just as they were when they were written. Thus, we do not as a rule hear of the later works of Haydn and Mozart being "arranged."[1] A few other works of the 'eighties and 'nineties which are still played—by such as Cherubini and one or two others—are generally left unaltered; and there is not the slightest reason why it should be otherwise.

Of the works written in the 'fifties, 'sixties and 'seventies, not very many are in the regular orchestral repertoire. The earlier works of Haydn and Mozart, which crop up now and again, are generally played as they were written, but without the keyboard-backing which rightly belongs to them and was part of their original make-up. The later works of Gluck require no arranging or re-orchestrating; a few of these are now played, sometimes as they were written, and sometimes re-orchestrated in a rather later style. A few other works of the same period are occasionally

---

[1] Arrangements for small or incomplete orchestras, school orchestras, military bands, etc., are in another category. They serve a definite and useful purpose, even if it is only that they bring the music within the range of many who otherwise would never play or hear it.

played; when these are performed exactly as written, but
without the keyboard-harmony which the composers counted on
having when they wrote them, they are in danger of being
misrepresented, and may sound hollow-centred, or, as it is
sometimes described, "all top and bottom." Relying on the
keyboard-harmony, the composers took little or no trouble to lay
out the string parts in such a way that the harmony would be
fully sounded by the orchestra. Harmony which might easily
have been complete is left incomplete; the second violins only too
often follow the firsts in unison, and the violas more often than
not duplicate the bass part in octaves. Neither the uppermost nor
the bass parts needed reinforcing, yet they are over-generously
supplied with tone, while the rest is left to the keyboard-instrument, possibly aided by a thinly disposed harmony on the oboes
and horns.

Such works can be played, just as they were written, by small
orchestras when a harpsichord is used as it was intended to be
used; the balance is then quite satisfactory. But when played in
the same way by large orchestras in large halls, the balance is
upset and the music is very liable to be distorted. The ghostly
chords of the harpsichord are quite unable to cope with the
volume of tone from the bowed-string instruments; the uppermost and lowest parts overwhelm the shadowy harmony; they
predominate unduly and disproportionately; the effect is un-
satisfying to the listener and unfair to the composer. There is
also the difficulty that harpsichord and player are not always
available under ordinary conditions at the present time; the
piano is an unsatisfactory substitute, and in either case an arrangement of the figured bass part is almost sure to be required.

Many works of this period are neglected because there is no
quite satisfactory way of playing them under present conditions.
It is true many of them are musically weak, and not worth
reviving. It is also true that the lay-out of the parts varies
very much according to the composer. Some of them were
apparently quite indifferent towards orchestral effect, and were
satisfied with worn-out conventional methods. Others were
distinctly interested in orchestral effect, as, for example, Gluck,
Piccinni and Gossec. Our own Arne could write well and badly
for the orchestra, and did both. The Mannheim symphonists
made more of their orchestration than did the contemporary
Italian opera manufacturers. But nearly all suffered from the

fact that they worked during the period of transition fron the age of the *basso continuo* to the age when the orchestra finally discarded the harmonic support of a keyboard-instrument.

A little judicious re-arrangement of the inner string parts can help those composers who were unfortunate enough to work just before the orchestra learned to stand on its own legs. The second violin and viola parts can be so placed that they supply the necessary harmony without robbing the top part and the bass of their due quantity of tone; they can be made to supply what the keyboard-instrument gave only with increasing inefficiency as time went on, and it can be done without interfering with the character, the style, or the colour of the music. In this way the balance of tone can be rectified so as to suit orchestras both large and small, and the problem of the keyboard-instrument is done away with. The dangers of adopting this course arise when the arranger will show off his own skill by adding matter which does not belong to the music or its period, when he adds orchestral colour which is alien to it, or when in any way he attempts to bring the music or the orchestration up-to-date. It is not up-to-date music, and nothing can make it so.

The purist, of course, will have none of this arranging, and there is something to be said for his view. The dangers mentioned above may possibly outweigh the disadvantages of the faulty balance and the problem of the keyboard-instrument; and once the arranger gets to work, who knows how far he will go. Undoubtedly, these arrangers need looking after.

When we come to the orchestral music written in the first half of the 18th century, the same problems present themselves, but are further aggravated by the fact that the composers of that time relied still more on the harmonic backing supplied by keyboard or chordal instruments. But here it is necessary to make a distinction between the music which was "worked-out" (*gearbeitete musik*,[1] as the old German musicians called it) and that which was not worked-out. The former is generally four-part writing of a contrapuntal texture, music which, in fact, could not be other than worked-out. Anything written in that way supplies its own harmonic structure. Although in its day it was always given the support of keyboard-harmony, such support is not essential, and it is not missed when it is not provided. Such music can now be played by any orchestra, large or small, which has

[1] "*gearbeitete Sachen, contrapuncte, fugen, u.s.w.*" (C. P. E. Bach).

F*

properly balanced string parts, and it is not only unnecessary to arrange or re-orchestrate it, but to do so is likely to misrepresent it and tear it out of its proper setting.

When the music was not worked-out; when it was written only in essential outlines, and no attempt was made to present the complete harmony by means of written parts, either the original keyboard-backing must be restored to it, or parts must be added which will complete the harmony. Almost any old opera, oratorio or cantata will provide examples of music which was written in such a way, as a melodic skeleton without harmonic flesh and blood. The vocal part of an aria and its bass may be all that is written down; a melodic violin part may be included in the scheme, or an *obbligato* part for some solo instrument, or for two; a few imitative or echoing phrases may be written, or some essential feature for one or two instruments may appear in the score when it is required; but the music is not complete if only these written notes are sung and played. Whether the bass part is actually figured or not, the whole thing was sounded against a background of chords played on either a harpsichord, an organ, or some other chordal instrument, it might be a lute, theorbo or harp. Similarly, in instrumental movements, in concertos, and even in overtures or symphonies, it may be that only the principal melodic part and the bass part are fully written out; or possibly two melodic parts acting in partnership at some distance above the bass part. But these are only the essential melodic outlines of the music, the framework which was intended to be clothed with harmony built up on the bass part, but not actually written down on paper.

There is also in these earlier scores a lot of three-part writing which is harmonically incomplete. Essential notes may be missing at any moment when the incidence of the written parts does not happen to represent the full harmony; and if only these written parts are played, the music sounds starved and hungry. The thin lay-out of the parts requires the assistance of completed harmony to bind it together and turn it into a cohesive whole.

This unworked-out music can be adequately presented, as it was in the days when it was written, by using a harpsichord, provided the orchestra is small enough to get sufficient support from that instrument, and provided the place where it is played is not too large for that instrument to be properly heard. Otherwise, if the tone of the orchestra dwarfs that of the keyboard-instrument and reduces it to a mere faint tinkle which only emerges now and again as if in timid protest, the music sounds hollow and ill-balanced, a naked structure without sufficient clothing.

When the use of a harpsichord is not feasible, or when the support it can give is insufficient, the essential harmony can be provided by re-laying-out the string parts in such a way that they take the place of the keyboard-harmony. In this way the balance of tone can be re-established, and the arrangement suits large or small orchestras, playing in large or small places, equally well. The addition of unobtrusive string tone does not add any alien colour to the music, and it should not impose on it any features which are not native to its style and period. Such an arrangement does not amount to re-orchestration; the process consists of little more than the addition of (possibly) second violin and viola parts to take the place of the harpsichord chords; it is really only doing what the composer himself would have done if he had chosen to "work-out" his music instead of leaving it in skeleton-form. To present the music without its essential harmony is to misrepresent it just as much as when fresh matter and colour is added to it. We have no right to over-dress our 18th century composers; but, on the other hand, we have no right to present them as nudists.

The entire re-orchestration of the earlier 18th century music is quite another matter. This may mean, and generally does mean, giving the music 19th century or even 20th century colouring. We have apparently easy consciences where re-orchestration is concerned, and are not particularly consistent. We frown on re-orchestrations of Bach,[1] but cheerfully accept Handel decked out in 19th century orchestration. Bach must retain his powdered wig and 18th century costume, but Handel may be dressed up in a frock coat and top hat. As for the lesser composers of the same period, they may be treated with even less consideration. They may be clothed in peg-top trousers or crinolines, in flannel bags and sports coats, in plus-fours or shorts. Who cares? There is no moral code to protect them against the assaults of the arranger, the adaptor, or the modern composer who may torture their simple tunes with the harmony of the moment, or perhaps

---

[1] An exception is made in the case of the Air from the orchestral Suite in D, better known as the "Air on the G string." This is reckoned fair game for any arranger.

only ape their manners on the plea that he is writing in a classical style. The musical arranger is no respecter of persons or of periods, and is allowed to do things the equivalent of which would be howled down if they were perpetrated in pictorial or architectural art.

Yet another type of arrangement is that in which 18th century music conceived for and written for a keyboard-instrument is transcribed for orchestra, with or without modern trimmings. There seems to be no urgent need for those transcriptions. If they must arrange, there is enough 18th century orchestral music still untouched to keep our arrangers busy for many years to come.

There exist to-day, side by side, both earnest efforts to restore 18th century music to its original condition and the most wilful attempts to distort and caricature it.

A back-to-the-land tendency which seeks to render the old music just as it was rendered in its own time is growing, and deserves encouragement even if only because it helps to protect the music against maltreatment, and against methods of presenting it which are inconsistent with its style and period. By all means let us have the parts which were written for the recorder played on that instrument, and the harpsichord brought back to its rightful place in the orchestra when it can be done without upsetting the balance of tone. But the most ardent advocate of the back-to-the-land movement must temper his enthusiasm with common sense, and recognise that it is impossible to get back to the land completely and with both feet. Time has passed, and with it some of the conditions which prevailed in the 18th century have passed away for ever. There are some features of 18th century performing methods which cannot now be recovered, and some which we would not restore even if we could do so.

The technique, method and style of playing bowed string instruments have undergone much change since the days of Vivaldi, Tartini, Leclair, Gaviniés, Benda and Stamitz. We can hardly hope to recover the many styles of violin-playing which were current in the 18th century, even if we were quite sure that we could distinguish between them. Changing technique has involved alterations to the necks, bridges and fingerboards of the instruments, and to the way they were held.[1] The bow, too, assumed its present form only towards the end

[1] The chin was formerly placed to the right of the tail-piece.

of the 18th century; before then it had been shorter, stiffer, and inclined to bend away from the hair instead of towards it. Burney tells of a 'cello player at Berlin who as late as 1772 held his bow "in the old manner, with the hand under the bow."[1]

These changes were accompanied by, or were brought about by developments which have considerably changed the technique, the style, and probably the tone of string instruments. We can hardly hope, or want, to go back to the less efficient and obsolete features of 18th century string playing. The playing of a string orchestra at the present time cannot sound quite the same as it did some 200 years ago, and even if we could recapture the sounds of those distant days it is most unlikely that we should be altogether pleased with them. If we wish to recover completely the playing of the mid-century string orchestra, we should, of course, have to get back some of those seedy viola players that Quantz wrote about, as well as those bungling double-bass players who skipped every alternate semiquaver in the quick passages and made scratchy noises with their bows.

An out-and-out back-to-the-land movement would mean laying aside, for the performance of 18th century music, all our nice modern wind instruments, with their mechanical facilities and improved intonation. The parts would have to be played on boxwood wood-wind instruments with a minimum of keys, and on valveless brass instruments. We do not need the testimony of Scarlatti, Quantz, Burney or Hawkins[2] to tell us that the wind instruments of their times were out of tune. When we examine the old flutes, oboes, clarinets and bassoons, we can see for ourselves where the finger-holes were bored, their size, how the instruments were tuned, and how their scales were produced. We can restore the old instruments and play them if necessary, or we can re-construct them on the old models, and the results will confirm our worst fears.

The difficulties which would be encountered and the results which would be achieved if the players of to-day were required

---

[1] Present State (Germany), II, p. 219.

[2] "My son, you know that I hate wind instruments, they are never in tune" (Scarlatti).

"The flute has the natural fault, that some of the sharpened notes are not quite in tune" (Quantz).

"The defect, I mean, is the want of truth in the wind instruments. I know it is natural to those instruments to be out of tune" (Burney).

The German flute "still retains some degree of estimation among gentlemen whose ears are not nice enough to inform them that it is never in tune" (Hawkins)

to play the earlier 18th century horn and trumpet parts on valve-less instruments would surely damp the enthusiasm of the most ardent back-to-the-lander.

A few other snags would include: the interpretation of the ornaments and small notes in the parts according to their correct French, German or Italian styles of the various periods; the improvisation of arbitrary embellishments in the solo parts and the addition of the proper cadenzas; the recovery of niceties of style which time has completely obliterated; lost traditions and customs; and above all, the adoption of a standard of taste which now no longer holds good.   No; the way of the musical back-to-the-lander cannot be an easy one unless he is prepared to make use of some of the improvements and amenities of a later age.   After all, we do like to have modern sanitation in our Georgian houses.

*   *   *

Apart from what they played, it is hardly possible to contem-plate 18th century orchestras without wondering *how* they played. We naturally ask ourselves: What did it all sound like? and, almost inevitably, a comparison is sure to creep into our curiosity: How would their playing compare with that of a modern orchestra?

Too much time has passed for memory or tradition to help us in answering such questions; we can do little more than wonder and speculate.   Contemporary opinions give us little or no help, for, even if we could reconstruct all the conditions under which the 18th century musicians played, we can never recover the standard by which their playing was judged in their own times.

We can, of course, set up some sort of relative standard, and distinguish between the playing of one 18th century orchestra and another.   We may be fairly confident, for example, that Karl Theodor's "army of generals"[1] at Mannheim played much better than the Bishop's odd assortment of seven musicians, nine servants in livery, a valet and a confectioner, at Grosswardein.[2]

We cannot doubt but that the King of Poland's famous orchestra at Dresden gave better performances than did Bach's little collection of *Stadtpfeifer* and amateurs at Leipzig.[3]   But we cannot find any common standard by which to compare the play-ing of Hasse's orchestra at Dresden in 1750 with that of the London Sympharmonic Orchestra under the baton of Sir Henry Thomas in 1940, nor can we measure the playing of the Leipzig

[1] Burney.   [2] Dittersdorf, p. 144.   [3] Terry, Bach's Orchestra, p. 9.

Stadtpfeifer against that of the present Municipal Orchestra at Eastmouth-on-Sea. Of course, we know perfectly well that Sir Henry Thomas' men would leave Signor Hasse's at the starting post, and that the orchestra at the well-known seaside resort would knock the old Leipzig *Stadtpfeifer* into a cocked hat. We may be equally positive that the B.B.C. orchestra, Section Z, under the direction of Mr. Nobody-in-particular, gives a better performance of Haydn's London Symphony than was secured by Haydn himself seated at the pianoforte in the Hanover Square Rooms. Yet, how can we substantiate any of these statements? The best we can do is to collect, from the evidence that has already been produced, every feature which seems to bear on the actual playing of the old orchestras, and base our conclusions on the story that they tell.

As regards the technical efficiency of the players, it is tolerably certain that only a few of the very best orchestras in the 18th century enjoyed the services of fully competent players throughout their ranks. Soloists and leaders were generally proficient, but there was a falling off amongst the rank and file. When Burney called the Mannheim orchestra an "army of generals," he was drawing attention to something quite exceptional and worthy of special remark. What has been said about the status of players (p. 85) seems to confirm this impression. Dittersdorf's evidence clearly points to inequality of technical skill amongst his musicians, and Bach's players at Leipzig were obviously not all first-class men. There is a suggestion of unequal efficiency in the distinction made between *Kammervirtuosen* and *Hof-musiker*, and in the presence of probationers (*accessisten*) in the German court orchestras. That so many players were double-handed, playing both string and wind instruments, also points to a standard rather below the best. A paragraph by Quantz, written about the middle of the century, after experience in Germany, France, Italy and England, may be quoted to show that shortcomings in the lower ranks of orchestras were very general rather than exceptional: "When one regards the conditions prevailing in most orchestras, whether attached to courts, republics or towns, one finds that imperfections in the accompaniment, which are especially due to the unequal skill of the players, are so considerable that one would hardly believe it to be possible unless one had actually experienced it."[1]

[1] *Versuch*, XVII, par. 4.

To the indictment must be added the general inferiority of the viola and double-bass playing which has already been noted.[1] Attention has also been drawn to the faulty intonation of the old wood-wind instruments. This seems to have been regarded as a natural imperfection peculiar to this type. The fact was evidently accepted with calm resignation; the instruments were out of tune; God made them so; well, it was a pity, but it couldn't be helped, so it was no good making a fuss about it. Moreover, the same trouble existed everywhere, as Burney told us: "this imperfection is so common to orchestras in general, that the censure will not be very severe on this (the Mannheim orchestra), or afford much matter for triumph to the performers of any other orchestra in Europe."[2]

As far as facility of execution on the wood-wind instruments of the 18th century is concerned, little more can be said but that we know the parts written for them, and we know what the contemporary instruments were like. Was there a race of super-players in those days who could play these parts perfectly on such primitive instruments? or did they just muddle through them as best they could? Again, we can only speculate and wonder. No doubt the technique was carried as far as was humanly possible, and one has only to read Quantz's tutor to know that the most conscientious players spent their lives in trying to overcome the difficulties which beset them, but with what result, no one can say. If the dried-up old instruments could speak, they could tell us all about it; but they are silent, and we have no gramophone records of Quantz playing one of his 300 flute concertos, or of Fischer playing his "celebrated rondo" for the oboe, as he did at Vauxhall Gardens. All these famous wind-players wrote and played concertos by the dozen, so they must have given some pleasure to their auditors; but would they have pleased our fastidious ears? Probably not.

There is no reason to suppose that the later 18th century horn and trumpet parts could not be played quite well on the natural instruments, although there must have been an occasional jar when a trumpet player tried to pass off his seventh open note as a B flat, or his eleventh open note as a good F or F sharp.[3] On the brass instrument playing in the first half of the century we must

---

[1] See pages 123, 143.   [2] Present State (Germany), I, p. 97.
[3] See Burney, History (reprint), II, p. 801; also, An Account, p. 87, and Parke, I, p. 41.

again fall back on speculation. Were the notes of those high and florid trumpet and horn parts poured out in a sweet limpid stream, in tune, perfectly controlled and articulated? or did they sometimes misfire, wobble, and fall over one another in an agonised scramble? Is there not in Burney's remark (1785) a faint hint that a certain amount of roughness was tolerated: "composers were not so delicate in writing for trumpets and French horns as at present," and in Mattheson's (1713) words: "screeching trumpets"?[1] Who can tell? Perhaps on the Day of Judgment we shall know. Those who like to enshroud the great composers of the 18th century in a cloak of perfection will not believe that anything but the most perfect playing would have satisfied their heroes, but those who know the brass instruments of the past, and the parts which were written for them, cannot help wondering whether these composers just accepted the vagaries of intractable and imperfect instruments as a part of their nature, and because they had never known anything better.

The efficacy of the old methods of controlling an orchestra, by means of keyboard or violin-direction, has already been discussed in Chapter IV. The conclusion reached was, that a fairly good standard of performance could be achieved provided the orchestra was small, not too widely scattered, and when all the players were equally efficient. We have seen that the last proviso would not apply to most 18th century orchestras, and we know that the best of these orchestras were not very small (Chapter II). We have also the evidence of Mattheson, C. P. E. Bach, Quantz, Junker and others, to show that difficulties did arise over the *ensemble*, and from the "Biedermann" and Reichardt we know that these problems were becoming more acute towards the end of the 18th century when orchestras were growing in size, and when orchestration was developing.

Taking all the foregoing data into consideration, and allowing for the facts that musicians were always playing music which was technically easy and of which every note would be heard, the general conclusion must be—that the standard of orchestral performance in the 18th century was such as would hardly be tolerated at the present time.

[1] "*Schreyende Clarinen*," Neu eröffnetes Orchester, par. 7.

BIBLIOGRAPHY

Adam, A. Derniers souvenirs d'un musicien. Paris, 1859.
Adlung, M. J. Anleitung zu der musikalischen Gelahrtheit.
Erfurt, 1758.
Agricola, J. F. Anleitung zur Singkunst. Berlin, 1757.
Almanach historique du Théâtre ou Calendrier historique et chronologique de tous les Spectacles. Paris, 1751–1801.
Ancelet. Observations sur la musique, les musiciens et les instruments.
Amsterdam, 1757.
Anon. Bemerkungen eines Reisenden über die zu Berlin vom 1787 bis 1788 gegebene Musiken. Halle, 1788.
  „ Briefe, zur Erinnerung an merkwürdige Zeiten. Berlin, 1778.
  „ (Einem teutschen Biedermann.) Wahrheiten die Musik betreffend. Frankfurt, 1779.
Bach, C. P. E. Versuch über die wahre Art das Klavier zu spielen.
Part I, Berlin, 1753; Part II, 1762. Modern reprint, Leipzig, 1906.
Berlioz, H. Les Soirées de l'Orchestre. Paris, 1854.
English trans., London, 1929.
Blandford, W. F. H. Handel's horn and trombone parts. Musical Times, Dec., 1939.
Brenet, M. Les concerts en France. Paris, 1900.
Brosses, Ch. de. Le Président de Brosses en Italie. Lettres familières écrites d'Italie en 1739 et 1740. 2nd Ed., Paris, 1858.
Burney, C. An Account of the Musical Performances in Westminster Abbey and the Pantheon . . . in Commemoration of Handel.
London, 1785.
  „ A general History of Music. 4 Vols.
London, 1776, 1782, 1789.
Reprint, 2 vols, London, 1935.
  „ The Present State of Music in France and Italy.
2nd Ed., London, 1773.
  „ The Present State of Music in Germany, the Netherlands and United Provinces. 2nd Ed., London, 1775.
Busby, T. A Dictionary of Music.
1st Ed., London, 1786; 4th Ed., 1813.
Carse, A. The History of Orchestration. London, 1925.
Castil-Blaze. De l'Opéra en France. Paris, 1820.
Chrysander, F. Der Bestand der königlichen Privatmusik und Kirchenkapelle in London von 1710 bis 1755. (Abdr. aus der Vierteljahrsschr. f. Mus.—Wiss. 1892, Heft 4.)
Cramer, C. F. Magazin der Musik. Hamburg, 1783, 1784.

Cucuel, G. Études sur un Orchestre au XVIIIme siècle.
Paris, 1913.
" La Pouplinière, et la musique de chambre au XVIIIe siècle.
Paris, 1913.
Denkmäler Deutscher Tonkunst. (Bavaria), 3rd year, Vol. 1.
Diderot-Alembert, Encyclopédie. Paris, 1767.
Dittersdorf, K. von. Autobiography. English trans., London, 1896.
Dörffel, A. Geschichte der Gewandhausconcerte zu Leipzig, 1884.
Fester, R. Die Bayreuther Schwester Friedrich des Grossen.
Berlin, 1902.
" Hohenzollern Jahrbuch. 1902
Forkel, J. N. Musikalischer Almanach für Deutschland.
Leipzig, 1782–84.
Forsyth, C. Orchestration. London, 1914, 1922.
Francœur, L. J. Traité général des voix et des instruments d'orchestre
Paris, 1772.
Führmann, M. H. Musikalischer Trichter. 1706.
Fürstenau, M. Zur Geschichte der Musik am Hofe der Kurfürsten von
Sachsen zu Dresden. Dresden, 1861–62.
Gassner, F. S. Dirigent und Ripienist. 1844.
" Universal-Lexikon der Tonkunst. Stuttgart, 1849.
Gerber, E. L. Historische Biographische Lexikon der Tonkünstler.
Leipzig, 1790–92.
Gradenwitz, P. Johann Stamitz.
Brünn—Prague—Leipzig—Vienna, 1936.
Grétry, A. E. M. Mémoires ou Essais sur la Musique.
Paris, 1789, 1797.
Grillet, L. Les Ancêtres du violon et du violoncelle. Paris, 1901.
Grimm, F. M. Le petit prophète de Boehmischbroda. 1753.
Grove, G. Dictionary of Music and Musicians.
3rd Ed., London, 1927.
Gunn, T. The School of the German Flute. London, 1794.
Gyrowetz, A. Selbstbiographie. Vienna, 1847.
Hammerich, A. Musiken ved Christian den Fjerdes Hof.
Copenhagen, 1892.
Hanslick, E. Geschichte des Concertwesens in Wien. Vienna, 1869.
Hawkins, J. A General History of the Science and Practice of Music.
London, 1776.
Hiller, J. A. Anweisung zum Musikalisch richtigen Gesang. 1774.
" Wöchentliche Nachrichten und Anmerkungen die Musik
betreffend. Leipzig, 1766–70.
Jahn, O. W. A. Mozart. Leipzig, 1867.
Junker, C. L. Einige der vornehmsten Pflichten eines Kapellmeisters
oder Musikdirectors. Winterthur, 1782.
" Musikalischer Almanach. Freyburg, 1782, 1783, 1784.
" Zwanzig Componisten. 1776.
Kastner, G. Traité général d'Instrumentation. Paris, 1836.
Kelly, M. Reminiscences. 2nd Ed., London, 1826.

Kleefeld, W. Das Orchester der Hamburger Oper, 1678–1738. (Sammelbände der I.M.G.)

„ Das Orchester der ersten deutschen Oper, Hamburg, 1678–1738.
Berlin, 1898.

Klob, K. M. Drei musikalische Biedermänner.   Ulm, 1911.

Koch, H. C. Musikalisches Lexikon.   Frankfurt, 1802.

Köchel, L. Die Kaiserliche Hof-Musikkapelle in Wien von 1543–1867.
Vienna, 1869.

Kolb, A. Mozart.   Eng. trans., London, 1939.

Küchelbecker. Allerneuste Nachricht vom kaiserliche Hofe. 1732.

Ledebur, K. Tonkünstler-Lexikon Berlins.   Berlin, 1860–61.

Löhlein, G. S. Anweisung zum Violinspielen.   2nd Ed., 1781.

Majer, J. F. B. K. Neu eröffneter theoretisch-praktischer Musik-Saal.   Nürnberg, 1732, 1741.

Marpurg, F. W. Die Kunst das Clavier zu spielen.   1750–51.

„ Historisch-Kritische Beyträge zur Aufnahme der Musik.
Berlin, 1754–57.

Mattheson, J. Exemplarische Organisten-Probe.   1719.

„ Neu eröffnetes Orchester.   Hamburg, 1713.

„ Der vollkommene Kapellmeister.   1739.

Mennicke, C. Hasse und die Brüder Graun als Symphoniker.
Leipzig, 1906.

Mizler, L. C. Musikalischer Staarstecher.   Leipzig, 1739–40.

Mozart, L. Versuch einer gründlichen Violinschule.
Augsberg, 1756.
Modern facsimile reprint, Vienna, 1922.

Mozart, W. A. (Emily Anderson). The letters of Mozart and his family.   London, 1938.

Nikolai, F. Beschreibung einer Reise durch Deutschland und die Schweiz im jahre 1781.   Berlin and Stettin, 1783.

Parke, W. T. Musical Memoirs.   London, 1830.

Petri, J. S. Anleitung zur praktischen Musik. Leipzig, 1782.

Pohl, C. F. Mozart und Haydn in London.   Vienna, 1867.

Quantz, J. J. Versuch einer Anweisung die Flöte traversiere zu spielen.   Berlin, 1752.
Partial reprint, Leipzig, 1906.

„ Autobiography (Marpurg's Beyträge, I, p. 197.)

Raguenet, F. Parallèle des Italiens et des François en ce qui regarde la Musique et les Opéras.   Amsterdam, 1704.

„ A comparison between the French and Italian Musick and Operas.   London, 1709.

Reichardt, J. F. Briefe eines aufmerksamen Reisenden. 1774–76.

„ Über die Pflichten des Ripienviolinisten.   Berlin, 1776.

Rochlitz, J. F. Anekdoten aus Mozart's Leben. Allgemeine Musikalische Zeitung.   Leipzig, 1799.

Rockstro, W. S. The Life of George Frederick Handel. London, 1883

Roeser, V. Essai d'instruction à l'usage de ceux qui composent pour la clarinette et le cor avec des remarques sur l'harmonie à deux clarinettes, deux cors et deux bassons.   Paris, 1764.

Rolle, C. K. Neue Wahrnehmungen zur Aufnahme und weiteren Ausbreitung der Musik. Berlin, 1784.

Rousseau, J. J. Dictionnaire de Musique.
Paris, 1756. Amsterdam, 1768.

Scheibe, J. A. Critischen Musicus. 1737–40.

Schneider, L. Geschichte der Kurfürstl. Brandenburg und Kgl. preussischen Kapelle. Berlin, 1852.

Schubart, C. F. D. Ideen zu einer Aesthetik der Tonkunst. (Written 1784–5, first pub. Vienna, 1806.)
Reprint, Leipzig, 1924.

Schünemann, G. Trompeterfanfaren, Sonaten und Feldstücke. (Reichsdenkmale Deutscher Musik. Abteilung einstimmige musik. Band I.) Kassel, 1936.

Schünemann, G. Geschichte des Dirigierens. Leipzig, 1913.

Spohr, L. Autobiography. Eng. trans., London, 1878.

Terry, C. S. Bach, a biography. London, 1928.

„ Bach's Orchestra. London, 1932.

Thayer, A. W. Ludwig van Beethoven's Leben. 1910–11.

Travenol, L, et J. Durey de Nionville. Histoire du théâtre de l'Académie Royale de Musique en France. Paris, 1757.

Türk, D. G. Klavierschule. Leipzig, 1789.

Walter, Fr. Geschichte des Theaters und der Musik am Kurpfälzischen Hofe. Leipzig, 1898.

Walther, J. G. Musikalisches Lexikon oder Musikalische Bibliothek.
Leipzig, 1732.

Wolf, G. F. Unterricht im Clavierspielen. Göttingen, 1783.

Wroth, W. The London Pleasure Gardens in the XVIII century.
London, 1896.

INDEX